FORBIDDEN
CHANNELS

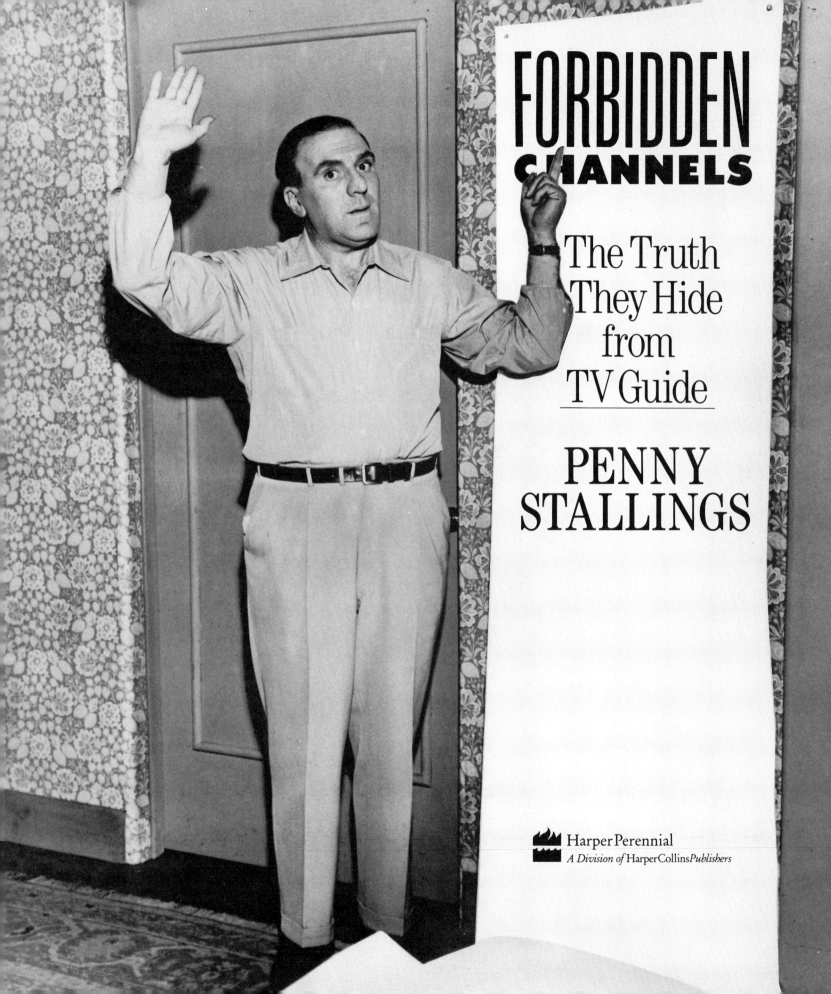

FORBIDDEN CHANNELS

The Truth They Hide from TV Guide

PENNY STALLINGS

HarperPerennial
A Division of HarperCollins*Publishers*

FIRST EDITION

Photo Sources: Photofest, NBC, ABC, CBS, HBO, Viacom,
The Museum of Broadcasting, and The Museum of Modern
Art.

Library of Congress Cataloging-in-Publication Data

Stallings, Penny.
  Forbidden channels/Penny Stallings.
    p.   cm.
  ISBN 0-06-055143-7
  ISBN 0-06-096330-1 (pbk.)
  1. Television programs—United States—Miscellanea.
2. Television actors and actresses—United States—
Miscellanea. I. Title.
PN1992.9.S7   1991   89-46489
791.45'0973—dc20

91 92 93 94 95 MPC 10 9 8 7 6 5 4 3 2 1
91 92 93 94 95 MPC 10 9 8 7 6 5 4 3 2 1 (pbk)

CONTENTS

ACKNOWLEDGMENTS

Thanks to Jennifer Hull, William Shinker, Ron Mandelbaum, Ed Maguire, Barry Gillam, Michael Saltz, Nancy Collins, Jim Stein, Ira Gallen, Ann Beatts, Henry Fera, Joseph Montebello, Ron Harvey, Derrick Dancker and Daniel Turetsky at Wolff Computers, Peter Wallach at Pronobis, Linda Dingler, Rena Kornbluh, Lee Blumer, Patrick Dillon, Paul Gamarello at Eyetooth Design, Vicki Gold Levi, Paula Klaw, Warren Levy, Ron Simon, Rick Kot, Carol Green, Susan Morris, Raymond Stallings, Suzanne Stallings, Jim Fox, Howard Frank, Kate Olson, Julie Klapper, Robyn Peterson, Patricia Neighmond, Bebe Green, Bevin McGuire, Sally Bedell, Karen Mandebach, Robert Morton, Marty at Ad-link, Carolyn Hart, Ann Armbruster, Carol Sothern, Charlotte Sheedy, Paul Slansky, William Smart at the Virginia Center for the Creative Arts, Michael Patrick King, Mike Rowe, and Synde Salem Cohen.

Special thanks to my editor, Craig Nelson, who saved me from myself; Howard Mandelbaum, for being the supreme source of all media wisdom; Joan Peters and Peter Passell, for their generous support and real estate; Frank Rose, for his sanity; Rick Mitz, for the insight, inspiration, and xerox paper that got me started again; Beth Rashbaum, who brought it all together; and Barry Secunda, who makes everything happen.

Photo research and design by Penny Stallings. Photo research by Howard Mandelbaum, Henry Fera, and Ron Mandelbaum of Photofest.

INTRODUCTION

Does television breed violence? Is it a numbing and addictive drug? Is it destroying the fabric of society or bringing us closer together?

Who knows? Certainly not me.

And you won't catch me trying to figure any of it out either.

I'm part of the generation that grew up with the Tube, so, for me, television is a given—neither moral, nor immoral. I watch it because I love it; I love it because it's there.

There's no way for me to separate my television-warped sensibility from what others might consider to be a reality-based view of the world. I am the sum total of a lifetime of television-watching and I track my past in terms of particular video benchmarks; it's impossible for me to separate my memories of adolescence from *American Bandstand* or the Beatles on *Ed Sullivan,* for instance, or those of my feminist awakening from *The Mary Tyler Moore Show* and *Dean Martin Presents the Golddiggers.*

It comforts me to know that I'm not alone, that it's that way for millions—particularly those of the Baby Boom Generation. Because television provides us with a collective reference point, its allusions can act as a kind of conceptual shorthand ("Oh Elaine, that dress is *very* Jetsons"). Writers of the TV generation use TV references to shape the way their characters perceive the world and how they tell their stories. And lately, we have even seen television embellishing and advancing its plotlines by invoking its own mythology. Michael Stedman on *thirtysomething* dreams he's Rob Petrie on an episode of *The Dick Van Dyke Show.* And Valerie Bertinelli tells a character on her new series, *Sydney,* that she sounds like something out of *One Day at a Time*—which was, of course, her old series, the one on which we watched her grow up. We the audience understand that this isn't just a throwaway joke, but a reference meant to summon up a specific image—in this case, a mother on her own raising a family. No other single source of metaphor is so rich or resonant for so many.

This book is for those who Get It, for those who have logged thousands of hours in front of the tube. Its focus then isn't on straight history or the content of television shows per se, but rather on what's going on just outside the frame, out of range of the camera's eye. Its organization is neither alphabetical nor chronological but by categories of my own devising —categories based on shared whimsy. On those occasions when direct reference is made to the content of the shows themselves, it will usually result from the intersection of small screen fiction and off screen weirdness—as with, say, the birth of Lucy and Desi's real-life and sitcom babies or the feuding between *Moonlighting*'s stars that made its way both into the tabloids and the show's sassy dialogue.

While some of the stories contained herein emanate from television's so-called Golden Era of live TV and kinescopes, most come from another, less-lauded golden era—the sixties and seventies—partly because so many of those shows are still very much with us and partly because of the now novel method in which they were logged into our memories (i.e., in their entirety, a practice that's fast becoming obsolete in this era of remote control grazing). Every so often a show—like *Murphy Brown* or *L.A. Law*—will inspire the whole country to sit down and watch it from start to finish (commercials included). But for the most part television viewing has become a matter of watching images flicker past in a giddy rush, as we zap from one channel to another.

Forbidden Channels also means to provide a visual record of a medium that, while itself visual, wasn't visually documented with any kind of consistency or wit. It wasn't television's fault: As a stepchild of the film industry, television didn't have the time or resources to polish its image or that of its stars in the Hollywood manner. It's only in the last decade that shows have been outfitted with such niceties as press kits complete with staged photo scenes and outtakes, and series stars have been packaged with glamour shots. Consequently it may be the most difficult of all the categories of the performing arts to illustrate with photos. Of course, that makes those photos that exist all the more precious for having been taken at all and, more amazingly, for having survived. I have juxtaposed some of those photos with folklore and TV-industry esoterica in order to give you a fresh take on those beloved old and new shows you've seen a million times before.

So now, let us travel together into that strange and bizarre world that lies beyond the dial, behind the box into the world of *Forbidden Channels* . . .

FORBIDDEN CHANNELS

TV GUIDE

Local Listings

November 22-28

15¢

WHAT'S THE PRICE OF AN ACTOR'S DIGNITY?

SEE PAGE 8

MLA

> Television—what a *horrible* way to make a living! Working in that medium is like working in a jungle. Everybody's out to get you if they can, and there's no one around to provide you with protection. I'll tell you this, it's not like it was in the old days when I was with MGM. That was the way to live!
> —Lana Turner

THE PRICE IS RIGHT

Okay, so maybe television was a comedown for Lana, but that didn't stop her from throwing her perfectly proportioned weight around on the few occasions she deigned to do it—for instance, as when Kevin McCarthy emerged as the critical favorite in her first series, *The Survivors* (1969), and Lana promptly ordered her bosses to cut his part. At forty-nine, Turner may not have been quite the force she once was in Hollywood, but she still packed a considerable wallop.

In fact, the only time Lana ever met her match in Televisionland was when she guest-starred on *Falcon Crest* opposite another Hollywood vet—Jane Wyman. Lana was popular with *FC*'s viewers, and she knew it, as her regal airs and hefty salary demands demonstrated. But although the show rose to the number-two position in the ratings after Lana joined it, Wyman nevertheless emerged the victor, seeing to it that Lana was banished after a brief stint. "I'll put up with a lot," Wyman said later. "But a limo to the loo is too much."

Joan Fontaine stars with **Mark Dana** in ''The Victorian Chaise-Lounge'' on The GE Theatre (1957).

14

Like Loretta Young in the old days and Angela Lansbury today, Wyman called the shots on *Falcon Crest*—just as she did on the old *Jane Wyman Show.* After all, somebody's got to. Directors, crew, and even cast members all come and go on a long-running hit, so it behooves the star of a weekly series to provide a sense of continuity (and to repel any possible encroachers on his or her turf). Screen divas like Wyman didn't get to the top of the old Hollywood star system by playing coy.

For those who don't play an offensive game, the results can be disastrous. Ask Dorothy Malone and the other seasoned senior players—Ruth Warrick, Ed Nelson, and George Macready—who were supposed to be the stars of *Peyton Place.* They were quickly eclipsed by newcomers Mia Farrow, Ryan O'Neal, and Barbara Parkins, who, for a while there in the mid-sixties, were accorded the kind of notoriety usually reserved for rock stars. Ambitious and self-involved, these young hotshots were oblivious, if not downright bratty, to everyone else (except, of course, to those with the power to further their careers).

The movie star on the home screen has always been a peculiar animal. And, then too, the relationship between film and TV got off to a rocky start right from the beginning, owing to the disdain felt for the upstart medium by everyone in the movie business (everyone who could afford it, that is). After the War, the powers controlling movies and radio treated television not as a stepchild, but as an orphan. Hollywood producers hoped that if they ignored TV, it would maybe just, you know, go away.

In 1952 the director of a live TV drama starring Lee Marvin miscalculated the time it would take his star to get from one scene—which was to close on him snuffing out a cigarette—to another in which he was to be shown making a call from a phone booth. The assistant director John Frankenheimer warned the director that the transition was uncomfortably tight, but the director held fast to his vision. The scene went reasonably well in dress rehearsal—with the camera hanging on the shot of the smoldering cigarette while Marvin ran to the phone booth as planned. But the director hadn't allowed for the rush actors get from live TV, nor for the fact that the studio they were in was on a sight incline and they were at the top of it . . .

Frankenheimer remembers: ''On air, they panned down to the ashtray, the cigarette was sizzling and Lee—because he was live—got this terrific burst of adrenaline and hit that phone booth at about twenty miles an hour. The booth then proceeded to roll across the studio verrry slowly. It was like a Fellini movie. We panned the phone booth across the studio, past the cameras; we even panned past an actress who was completely naked—changing for her next scene! And of course Lee was talking a mile a minute, but you couldn't hear anything he was saying because the boom was still where we left it. We kept panning with the phone booth till it finally hit the wall at the end of the studio!''

Many veteran stars were also openly hostile toward the primitive new medium. (Clark Gable not only refused to appear on television but went out of

Ann Sheridan stars with Steven Geray and Richard Egan in ''Malaya Incident'' on Ford Theatre (1953).

Ronald Coleman stars on Four Star Playhouse (1953).

15

his way to snub TV reporters.) Because programming was so brash and slapdash and, most of all, so very available, film stars feared that such exposure would diminish them in the eyes of their adoring (read ''ticket-buying'') public. Early televised images were grainy and unflattering, and it was next to impossible to look movie star glamorous in the thick, cakey makeup required for television's hot lights—so their fears weren't entirely unfounded.

Moreover, for actors accustomed to the multiple takes of movie-making, the get-it-right-the-first-(and-only-)time nature of live TV was a nightmare—or as Paulette Goddard once characterized it, ''a premiere on Broadway that closes after opening night.'' (Fortunately, Goddard didn't have to suffer such opening night jitters often, since a string of well-paying film roles and well-fixed husbands had left her extremely well heeled.)

But those film luminaries willing to swallow their trepidation (or their pride) and appear on TV helped make the fifties the most interesting of times on the small screen. Some even managed to thrive on the pressure of live TV, with the tension serving to make their performances electrifyingly kinetic. Myrna Loy

Claudette Colbert stars as a widow whose daughter (Eilene Janssen) suspects her of trying to steal her boyfriend in ''While We're Young'' on Ford Theatre (1955).

16

Margaret Sullavan rehearses a scene from ''State of the Union'' with Nina Foch and Joseph Cotten on <u>Producers' Showcase</u> (1954).

has spoken glowingly of the exhilaration that came from conjuring up a work of art practically on the spot. And Roddy McDowall credits the acting craft he has today to being forced to come through on live TV.

Not everyone was so sanguine. Paul Newman has said he's never been more afraid in his life than during his early days on live shows like *Producers' Showcase* and *The Alcoa Hour*. Back then, when an actor forgot his lines midscene, he would stand there helpless, his eyes raised heavenward, as he waited for someone . . . anyone . . . to take pity on him and whisper the next line. And, in fact, more than a few brilliant film actors dried up on live TV. On one memorable occasion, the legendary James Cagney went blank during a long and poignant speech about bringing bodies back home from overseas for burial during World War II. Ten heart-stoppingly long seconds

elapsed before he was able to pick up the thread.

Margaret Sullavan, the celebrated stage and screen actress, panicked before she ever got in front of the camera for a *Studio One* drama called ''The Pilot.'' Although an old hand at live TV, she quarreled with producers over the chaotic rehearsal schedule and the lack of time they'd given her to master the seventy-two props called for in the script. She calmly walked out on the production during a final run-through, leaving Nancy Kelly to replace her, and fled to a friend's country home without telling anyone (including her family) where she was—thereby leading to speculation that she'd been the victim of foul play (as opposed to a fit of thespian pique). The ensuing uproar caused the high-strung actress to suffer an apparent breakdown that culminated in a three-month-long stay in a sanitarium.

Greer Garson stars with Philip Reed in "The Earring" on The GE Theatre (1957).

Film actors weren't the only ones who froze in front of television's unblinking eye. Radio performers, used to reading their ad-libs directly from a script, also felt threatened by the high-wire nature of television work. And for stage performers accustomed to getting human feedback, the lack of audience response could be lethal. "I can't relax with all those technicians wandering back and forth," complained radio star Fred Allen of TV. "They listen to me tell the joke in rehearsals for two days, and by the time the performance rolls around, they're leaning on their cameras and staring at me with all the enthusiasm of a dead trout." Ed Wynn sized up the dilemma even more succinctly when he observed: "You can't get laughs out of a cameraman's ass."

All the obvious drawbacks aside, the relatively low production budgets of this new medium also meant that producers could afford to take chances. New material was in constant demand, and talented young writers who would ordinarily have had to wait months—or even years—for Broadway exposure found themselves constantly employed and, even

more miraculously, frequently produced. Paddy Chayefsky, Rod Serling, Gore Vidal, Tad Mosel, J. P. Miller, Reginald Rose, Horton Foote, James Costigan, and Robert Alan Aurthur were among the fresh talents with new ideas who fed the monster's insatiable appetite. Not only were there prime-time anthology shows like *Studio One* and *The Kraft Television Theatre* to supply, but there was also *Matinee Theatre,* which aired an hour-long dramatic show every weekday afternoon. Of course, for each "Marty" and "Requiem for a Heavyweight" there were numerous duds. But the immediacy and intimacy of live television made even those an adventure.

With the high caliber of the writing and the eventual improvements made in the technology, television became less and less threatening to performers' vanity, and eventually even managed to develop its own brand of glamour. The hundreds of live dramatic productions presented yearly were to prove a lifeline for those veteran stars for whom Hollywood's shrinking production schedules offered few opportunities. The public wouldn't go out of its way to see older stars at the movies, but it was an *occasion* when the

17

Barbara Stanwyck stars with Jeff Morrow in "Sudden Silence" on Ford Theatre.

Mary Astor plays a fading actress who is picked up on a drunk-driving charge and bailed out by a mystery man in "The Star" on The Lux Video Theatre (1956).

18

messed-up grown-up, a two-time loser in marriage with a huge alimony nut to cover. After several years of free-lance work in dismal features (*Francis in the Haunted House, The Atomic Kid,* etc.), he triumphed in a 1957 *Playhouse 90* production called "The Comedian"—a role he'd won by default after all of America's leading comic actors turned it down for fear of being identified with the leading character. Rooney was nominated for an Emmy and his name was golden again. "Suddenly everybody decided that Mickey Rooney knew how to act," he said. Although he didn't know it then, Rooney's film career was, for the most part, over; his most memorable adult performances—and there would be many—were to be on TV.

After the gradual demise of the anthology drama in the fifties, acting on TV came to mean, with periodic exceptions, the numbing drill of weekly series. While a good deal more lucrative than guest shots, such enterprises understandably looked like drudgery to pampered screen stars. They agreed to do them because they had no choice; it was either *The Beverly Hillbillies* or selling real estate in Beverly Hills.

very same stars appeared on a live television drama—something the viewing public would stay home to watch, then talk about excitedly at work or school the next day.

After a thirty-year-long career, Mary Astor was washed up in movies until a 1955 appearance on the half-hour suspense show *Danger* initiated a burst of activity. "The day following that show, I went into rehearsal for the *Producers' Showcase* production of 'The Philadelphia Story,' " she wrote later. "Less than a week after that, I began the Philco show, and the day after that I started rehearsal on 'The Thief' for *The U.S. Steel Hour*—and the following day I began on 'The Hickory Limb' for Ponds. A few days later I started three weeks' rehearsal on NBC's big color production of *The Women,* where I got into money. All of a sudden, I was what is known in the business as 'hot.' "

Mickey Rooney also managed to jump-start his stalled career by switching from movies to television. Once one of the most beloved child stars of the prewar years and one of MGM's biggest money earners, Rooney had returned from a stint in the army as a

Angela Lansbury and **Howard Duff** in "The Ming Lama" on Ford Theatre.

Bette Davis in "With Malice Toward One" on The GE Theatre (1957).

Ronald Reagan was one of many old line Hollywood names to take a strong stand against television —particularly during his early years as president of the Screen Actors Guild. But having been reduced to groaners like *Bedtime for Bonzo* and *Hong Kong* by the fifties (and damn few of those), Reagan had a change of heart in 1954 when he agreed to take on hosting (and occasional acting) chores for *The GE Theatre*. "I remember Ronnie telling all of us not to join TV because it was the enemy of the movies," Ann Sheridan said later. "Next thing he was on *GE Theatre* with his contact lenses reading the commercials."

Reagan was later bounced from *GE Theatre* after speaking at a fundraiser for Congressman John Rousselot of the John Birch Society. Apparently his off-camera political speeches were a mite too far to the right even for that conservative company's comfort. But Ronnie and television were a good match, and he would be back—first as the host of *Death Valley Days* and then as host to our nation for an endless stream of soporific presidential performances called "The Reagan Eighties."

Reagan's friend Frank Sinatra, though more conspicuously talented and charismatic, didn't fare nearly so well when he took to the air in 1950 with his first TV series—a weekly musical variety show. The bad boy quality that played so well in smoky saloons turned out to be a detriment in living rooms where Sinatra's innate surliness practically seemed to seep through the screen. But in all fairness, Ol' Blue Eyes had other things on his mind: Because his show was broadcast live from New York, Sinatra was forced to leave his young wife, Ava Gardner, back on the coast. The separations aggravated the couple's already volatile relationship, and with each passing week Sinatra grew increasingly obsessed with Ava and her well-documented wandering ways. In order to keep an eye on her, he flew back to Hollywood after every show, often returning to New York the day of broadcast, thereby missing or cutting short rehearsals and radically undermining quality. Sometimes it was all his producers could do to get a simple hour of him singing in front of a curtain. And then too, TV was a comedown for Sinatra, a bailout he'd resorted to because his career was floundering and he was tapped.

When another giant took to the small screen a few years later, it also had everything to do with money—or the lack of it. Judy Garland was even

19

Frank Sinatra runs through his song selection for a telecast of The Frank Sinatra Show (1957).

Could **Judy** make it through her number? Could we bear watching her try?

issued forth during each thrilling note. Could she make it through her scripted bits of business, the interplay with her guests, the show? Could we bear to watch? Of course we could. Truth to tell, we couldn't look away.

For a star like Garland, television's candor could be incredibly cruel, illuminating every flaw. Too real, too raw, it dismantled the elaborately crafted studio-created illusion so essential to her winsome allure. It was every established star's worst nightmare—the reason so many held themselves aloof if they could. But midway through the seventies, attitudes about TV began to soften in Hollywood circles as an increasing number of big names attempted to prolong their careers with weekly series. James Stewart, Henry Fonda, Yul Brynner, Doris Day, Shirley MacLaine were just a few. Yet, despite their solid gold status, their failure rate was surprisingly high—perhaps because of their continuing ambivalence about the medium.

For those who did prevail over the killing demands of a weekly series, the costs, as well as the rewards, could be mighty high. Angie Dickinson, while buoyed by the success of *Police Woman,* blamed the show for the demise of her marriage to composer Burt Bacharach. Others, like Robert Stack, managed to fend off the pressures of their series while at the same time dominating them. Although the putative star of *The Untouchables,* Stack would often quite literally phone in his part (particularly during the show's later years), mouthing Elliott Ness's clipped dialogue into a prop phone—and leaving the remainder of the episode to focus on the more colorful hoods and racketeers. And yet, however brief (and wooden) his presence, Stack gave *The Untouchables* continuity.

Henry Fonda's sheriff on *The Deputy* was frequently out of town on business (at Sheriff's conventions, maybe?), leaving young Allen Case to keep the town clean and memorize most of the show's stilted script. But because Fonda narrated all of the episodes whether he appeared in them or not, they retained his distinctive imprint.

Walter Brennan conserved his time and energy during his years on *The Real McCoys* by reciting his lines straight off the cue cards—much to the irritation of his co-stars, particularly the scrupulously professional Richard Crenna. As cranky as his TV alter ego, Brennan continually threatened to quit throughout the show's eight-year run, protesting that he couldn't do comedy. (The critics agreed.) By the show's fifth

more desperately in need of quick cash than usual when she agreed to do a television series in 1963— owing to a custody battle with Sid Luft over their two children, and also to a $50,000 blackmail fee she had recently paid for the return of a photograph taken at a London hospital that showed her with her stomach being pumped following a drug overdose.

Garland's show lasted only one year, but that year was mythic for those who were lucky—and masochistic—enough to suffer through it with her. Could she make it through her song? viewers wondered, as they watched the contortions of face and body that

Walter Brennan tells **Richard Crenna** how he feels about doing comedy.

be inserted into various episodes. All MacMurray had to do was change his cardigan and (maybe) his expression.

One of the few movie-star transplants to score a full-fledged television hit, Rock Hudson nevertheless managed to look down his nose at his TV work until almost the very end of his life. His series, *McMillan and Wife,* lasted for seven years, a period that he later characterized as sheer agony. Harboring the typical movie-star prejudice against TV, Hudson had turned down many series offers. He'd even criticized his close friend George Nader for stooping to TV work—despite the fact that, unlike him, Nader had no choice (if he wanted to continue acting). But drinking had taken its toll on Hudson's leading-man looks by the early seventies, and fewer romantic film leads were being offered to him. He finally relented when NBC offered him $120,000 per episode—the highest fee

season, Brennan had wangled a deal which required him to do only a few minutes of his arm-flapping, squawking Grampa Amos shtick in just half of the season's twenty-six episodes.

Brennan's sweet deal was nothing compared to the one finagled by Fred MacMurray on *My Three Sons.* The producers of that show had originally wanted to call it *The Fred MacMurray Show,* but its namesake objected—seeing as how "if your name is on a show, you have to be on it all the time." And MacMurray didn't want to be on the show all the time. He barely wanted to be on it *any* of the time. He did, however, want the full-time rewards of weekly prime time stardom so he got the show's producers to agree to certain concessions.

The *My Three Sons* scripts were written well in advance so MacMurray could shoot all his scenes for the year in sixty-five days. That meant that every scene from every script that took place in, say, the upstairs hallway was shot in an afternoon, out of sequence, one right after the other—so they could then

Don Grady and **Stanley Livingston** showed up for a tribute for their TV dad given by USC in 1989, but the indifferent **MacMurray** was not exactly beloved by his Three Sons.

"Why didn't I try harder," **Rock Hudson** (here with **Susan St. James**) asked his friends while watching old reruns of McMillan and Wife.

yet paid to an actor in TV. The deal was further sweetened with leading-lady and script approval.

Even with *McMillan*'s solid popularity, Hudson remained impossible to please. He didn't like the scripts and he didn't like the hours and he didn't like the low-rent status of working in TV, and his feelings were apparent in every painfully stiff scene he played. He managed to be professional—always on time, always on top of his lines—but he was anything but inspired. Off camera, he fortified himself with booze, often locking himself away for hours in his dressing room. His only pleasure seemed to be in needling his co-star: "Fuck the ecology," he'd taunt Susan Saint

James, who was at the time very much into her flower-child persona. "Let's pump more oil out of the ground."

Saint James had been Hudson's personal choice for the "and wife" role, and yet there had never been any real chemistry between the two—either on screen or off. Hudson remained cut off from her by both his old-guard star status and his sycophantic entourage. And then too, they were separated by a sizable generation gap: she was a sunny, funny Hollywood hippie and he was a man some twenty years her senior trying desperately to hold on to his youth with corny mod suits and blow-dried hair. Oddly enough, in everything but his freewheeling sex life, Rock Hudson was stodgy—an old-line conservative who counted both Nancy Reagan and the self-proclaimed homophobe John Wayne among his friends. That stodginess contributed not only to tensions on the set of *McMillan and Wife* but to the overall insipidity of the show.

To make matters worse, it was his flaky co-star who garnered the Emmy nominations for four years running while Mr. Movie Star got nary a nod. Saint James eventually departed after a contract dispute, leaving Hudson to finish up the show's run.

Although Hudson later scorned *McMillan and Wife* in interviews, he came to think better of the show toward the end of his life. Watching the reruns, he often expressed surprise that they weren't nearly as bad as he remembered. "Why didn't I put more into it?" he would ask himself and his friends.

Hudson's lifelong ambivalence toward television is just another instance of the edgy, grudging relationship that exists between film and TV to this day. Even at the ridiculously inflated salaries offered as series incentives, true superstars like Hoffman, Redford, Beatty, Keaton, Streep, or DeNiro wouldn't be caught dead on regulation TV. Oh sure, a big name might venture a "special TV event" in mid-career, but the halcyon era that saw movie stars popping up all over the dial is never to return. In other words, Jane Fonda may deign to do a TV movie of *The Dollmaker,* but don't expect her to show up as the host of *The Jane Fonda Theater* any time soon. (Not as long as she can do a passable leg lift, anyway.)

So, until the era of first-run theatrical release pay-for-play television becomes a reality, here's the reasonably steadfast rule: Random cameo roles and special events notwithstanding, movie stars just don't do television. Or rather, they don't do television until they can no longer do movies. And when they do, their presence doesn't necessarily guarantee a hit (sometimes just the opposite, it seems). Even so, we'll continue to see the occasional film star uneasily attempting to make the transition into television as long as mortgage payments on Beverly Hills mansions outlast big screen allure and the longing for the public's love persists in the hearts of the chosen.

In other words . . . forever.

23

Red Skelton, age 2.

ALL MY CHILDREN

Close your eyes.

Now imagine the following group shot: Robert DeNiro. Robert Conrad. Jane Fonda. Jane Seymour. Jack Nicholson. Jack Klugman. Meryl Streep. Mary Tyler Moore. William Hurt. William Shatner.

What's wrong with this picture?

They're all stars. Big ones. But some are movie stars and some are TV stars, and never (well, hardly ever) the twain shall meet. They may flit back and forth between the two mediums, but they remain solidly identified with one or the other.

So what's the difference between them? Is there some sort of genetic predisposition that destines an actor for the big screen as opposed to the small? Do they possess a different look? Different allure? Talent? Scale? Packaging? Yes, all that and more.

Whereas the big screen loves the strange and unusual, television enshrines the brazenly bland. Unlike their big screen counterparts, TV stars can't burn too brightly, can't be too intense. Oh sure, there are a few exceptions, but as a rule, the kind of personality that thrives best in the cool atmosphere of the cathode rays is low-keyed and nonthreatening. In this curious world, even the gorgeous are made interchangeable by insipid beauty contestant perfection, and ethnics have a tendency to become "white bread." Add to this cookie-cutter conformity the middle-American norm of unfailingly predictable behavior and you get stars who can certainly inspire affection—but awe—never!

Take those two television mainstays Dinah Shore and Bob Newhart. They comfort us because they don't challenge us too strenuously. And how about that paradigm of small screen charisma, Bill Bixby? Now there's someone you wouldn't look at twice at the mall, and yet he's been tapped to star in not one, not two, but *six* TV series during his long, impressive career. His rerun backlog is so vast that he is guaranteed to be on the air somewhere, on some channel, at some hour of each and every day from now until the end of the millenium. So, just what is it that has brought this seemingly unexceptional fellow into our homes for lo these many years? Does he radiate

Gracie Allen, age 6.

some sort of subtle magic that only the camera can see? Or is he simply the luckiest man in the world? Neither really. It's Bill Bixby's very ordinariness that assures his longevity on the small screen, that pumps up his perennially perky likability quotient, his "TV Q."

The most durable TV series stars project an Every(wo)man quality that enables us to identify with them, while screen stars tend to be bigger-than-life icons we worship from a distance. That's part of the reason it's so difficult for film stars to successfully make the jump to TV. Oh sure, it happens every so often, but almost always with those stars who haven't created indelible screen images. A star like Jimmy Stewart, for example, is too quirky, too distinctive to pare down his schtick for TV (although he's tried twice). By contrast, the regular-Joe quality that prevented Robert Young from becoming anything more than a serviceable first or second lead in films catapulted him to the top of the TV hierarchy in the fifties. The same principle applies to other successful movie-TV crossovers like John Payne, Jane Wyatt, and Donna Reed. Their ordinariness enabled them to communicate with audiences in an intimate way. The "real people" of the movies—character actors—also wear well with home viewers: William Bendix, Stu Erwin, Jack Webb, Jack Klugman, Phil Silvers, and Raymond Burr all went from supporting roles in the movies to leads on TV.

Buddy Ebsen was well on his way to becoming one of the screen's most beloved song-and-dance men when he nearly lost his life (and his career) after being poisoned by the aluminum dust used for his body makeup as the Tin Woodsman in *The Wizard of*

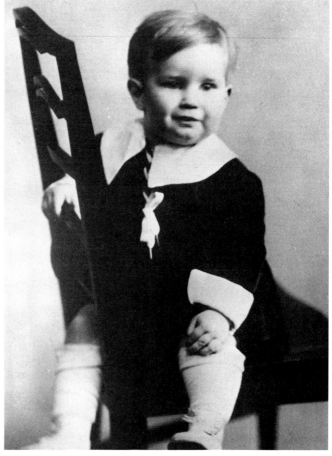

Charlton Heston, age 2.

Oz. But missing out on that legendary role saved him from the sort of permanent identification with a part that caused another of the Oz stars, Ray Bolger, to be forever enshrined in memory as the beloved Scarecrow. While Bolger would never enjoy such success again—either on the screen or on television, Ebsen's greatest triumphs lay before him. It would take years before he surfaced again with any kind of permanence, but when he finally did—as Fess Parker's sidekick on *Davy Crockett*—it marked the beginning of an astoundingly successful TV career that has had him starring in something or other ever since.

Lucille Ball is another who's lumped into the category of movie-star-turned-TV-star. But the truth is that Lucy's screen career—though long and active—never really ignited. (Think fast . . . what's *your* favorite Lucille Ball movie?) For all her much-touted terms at RKO and later MGM, most of what survives of Lucy on celluloid is a haughty figure encased in box-shouldered drag gliding indifferently through one dreary

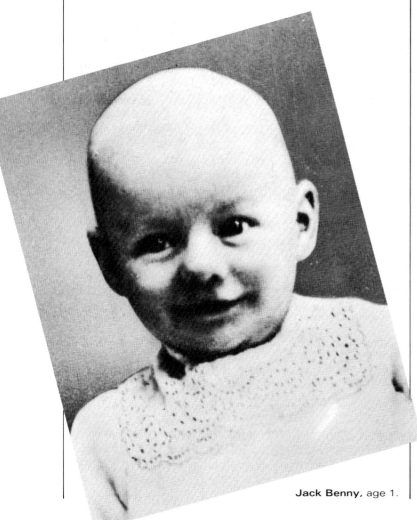

Jack Benny, age 1.

picture after another. It was radio that first released her comedic gifts, and it was television that allowed those gifts to blossom into full-blown genius, providing her with a happy ending escape from an industry that never took her seriously or used her well.

Like Ball, Candice Bergen had made dozens of movies, but she never really sparkled until she made the move to TV. Too straightforward, perhaps even too sane, to make sparks fly on the big screen, she hinted of her affinity only once, in *Starting Over,* as a songwriter whose narcissism and off-key singing foreshadowed the character traits she's managed to make so lovable as Murphy Brown.

If it's next to impossible for a major film star to make the transition to television, the reverse trip is even more unlikely. Tom Selleck is everything a movie star ought to be—tall, suave, and drop-dead gorgeous, but while he looms large on the small screen, he gets small on the big one—partly because of his week-to-week familiarity as Magnum P.I., and partly because it reveals him to have only one emotional note. (Okay, maybe two). That doesn't mean Hollywood won't continue to try to make use of him. But like John Ritter and Michael J. Fox, Tom Selleck will most likely remain a TV star who happens to make movies.

Sid Caesar, age 2.

27

Steve Allen, age 2.

Phyllis Diller, age 2.

Steve McQueen managed to escape the TV star trap by bolting *Wanted Dead or Alive* before becoming irrevocably identified with the show in the public mind. Itchy to bail out of the series almost from the moment he got a taste of the big time with his co-starring role in *The Magnificent Seven,* he managed to get out of his long-term contract by staging a car accident in which he slammed his rented Caddy convertible into a wall (severely injuring himself and his wife in the process).

Can you see Gavin MacLeod doing something like that? Or Betty White? Nope. It just doesn't figure. But that brings up another important difference between TV and movie stars: They are often as different in temperament as they are in everything else. Movie actors can get away with hiding from the public, with playing it cool and mysterious. But because television stars are regarded as virtual members of the family by their fans, they are required to submit themselves to public scrutiny almost as much as the stars of the studio era—but without benefit of the studio's careful shielding of the flesh-and-blood person behind the fabricated image. TV stars are required to open their homes, display their families, or pose in the occasional bathtub in much the same way movie stars did for *Photoplay* or *Modern Screen,* but they must also give us access to their most intimate life secrets, no matter how compromising. The TV audience wants its stars to be as ordinary, and as troubled, as the people next door.

28

Candice Bergen, age 5, with her father **Edgar** and her "brother" **Charlie McCarthy** (1951).

Rock Hudson, age 8.   **Patty Duke**, age 8.

Lawrence Welk, age 16.

Joan Rivers, age 14.

TV and movie stars differ in the degree—if not the nature—of their ambition, too. Movie stars (especially those of the twenties and thirties) were often the product of oppressive poverty, so their struggle had a real life-and-death edge to it. Happily, most actors are no longer haunted by the specter of adversity that motivated stars like Jean Harlow and Joan Blondell, who were the sole means of support for their large families during the mean years of the Depression. When *People* magazine does TV-star profiles you rarely get the old-fashioned horror stories. Sure, Joan Rivers's father once threatened to have her committed if she didn't abandon her acting ambitions and come home. But she was a well-to-do girl driven by the hunger for recognition, not the voracious craving for survival. For stars of the studio era a show business career was an all-or-nothing proposition. They didn't hedge their bets the way Marla Gibbs did during the first two years of *The Jeffersons,* during which she kept her job as an airline clerk while waiting to see if her future was secure.

While movie stars are otherworldly creatures, TV stars 'R' us . . . or we like to think they are anyway. Look deep into the faces of these Nielson Family children, and see if you can see the ordinary quality that makes them so special, and the magic that makes us believe that they're no different than us.

29

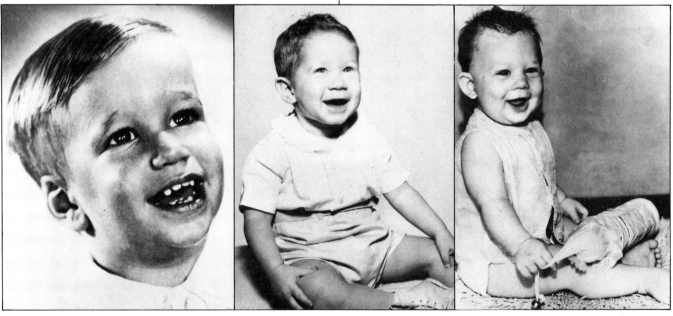

Henry Winkler, age 2.   **Donny Most**, age 2.   **Ron Howard**, age 2.

John Carson
Class of 1943
Norfolk Nebraska High school

Gilda Radner, age 16.

William J. Murray
Class of 1968
Loyola Academy

Dick Van Dyke, age 16.

Tom Selleck
Class of 1962
Grant High School

30

Morgan Fairchild

Don Johnson
(and friend)

Bruce Walter
"Buck" Willis

Louise Lasser

...rton (Sean) Downey, Jr. (left),
...h his parents and brother **Michael** (1936).

Carol Burnett, age 16.

THE YOUNG AND THE RESTLESS

It's four A.M. You're wide awake. You flip on the TV . . . a sure way to lull yourself back to sleep. You click from a monster truck rally to Gene Scott to an old *Andy Griffith* rerun—you know, the one where Aunt Bee gets called for jury duty. Ho hum, seen it before—might as well check back with monster trucks. But wait a minute . . . who's that guy playing the crook, the one Aunt Bee is so sure is innocent? It looks like . . . naw, too nerdy—too much hair. Wait a minute—it *is!* Imagine Jack Nicholson hanging out in Mayberry with Andy and Opie and Aunt Bee!

Few things in life are more satisfying than discovering a star in a bit part in an old movie or TV show —back before the nose job and the acting lessons, before discarding the Brooklyn accent (or, in the case of Robert Blake and Tyne Daly, before acquiring it).

Watching an old film or TV show can be like going on an archaeological dig as you scrutinize the faces of the supporting cast, mentally dusting away the years to discover a young Sylvester Stallone on *Kojak,* maybe, or Burt Reynolds on *The Twilight Zone.*

Yes, you can see them still, frolicking in old reruns, lurking in the shadows on *The Million Dollar Movie*—series favorites in old movies, movie stars in ancient TV. They'll be there waiting for you tonight after normal people have gone to bed. Warren Beatty on *Alfred Hitchcock Presents,* Elizabeth Montgomery in *The Untouchables,* and Carroll O'Connor on *The Man from U.N.C.L.E.* Of course, most of the kinescopes of the really early live dramas (with stars like Grace Kelly and James Dean) are too creaky to be rerun (that is, if they exist at all). And some of the movies—like *Kid Monk Baroni* with Leonard Nimoy —are so rickety they don't even rate a slot on *The Late Late Show.* Still, there are more than enough stars to be flushed out of their hiding places to make the hunt worthwhile. But until you've learned to track them yourself, allow me to reveal a few of them now —as they were then.

Even **Grace Kelly**—a star from the moment she decided to be one—paid her dues in stiff TV plays with cardboard sets and meandering props. She was one of a whole generation of actors who refined their skills in the catch-as-catch-can arena of live television.

Grace Kelly in ''Fifty Beautiful Girls'' on <u>Suspense</u>.

33

Johnny Carson with Jackie Laughery on <u>Earn Your Vacation</u> (1954).

The arty Actors Studio set were all over the dial in the early fifties—smoldering, brooding, suffering for their Art: James Dean in *Schlitz Playhouse of Stars,* Paul Newman on *Producers' Showcase,* and Anne Bancroft on *Studio One* and *The Alcoa Hour.*

34

James Dean did occasional TV work in between acting on stage and testing stunts on Beat the Clock. Here he appears (with Pat Hardy) in "The Unlighted Road" on Schlitz Playhouse of Stars in the spring of 1955—a few months before the release of East of Eden made him a world-class star.

A good deal less mannered than the brooding Brando clone who would soon take to the screen (in Somebody Up There Likes Me and The Long Hot Summer), **Paul Newman** was a fresh new presence in dramatic anthologies like the Goodyear and Philco playhouses in the early fifties—and particularly The U.S. Steel Hour's touching baseball fable "Bang the Drum Slowly." He even sang a duet with **Eva Marie Saint** in this Playhouse 90 adaptation of "Our Town" (1955).

Anne Bancroft and **Lloyd Bridges** in "A Time to Cry" on The Alcoa Hour.

For busy New York actors who played dozens of roles in a year's time, television provided a means of expanding one's range while learning how to deal with the pressure of getting it right the first (and only) time. It was a tightrope walk requiring spunk and inventiveness, what with unexpected occurrences like fluffs, missed cues, wobbly sets, or leftover air time.

Lillian Gish, Raymond Massey, and **Jack Lemmon** as John Wilkes Booth in "The Day Lincoln Was Shot" on The Alcoa Hour (1956).

Bruce Lee with Van Williams in The Green Hornet (1966).

Kurt Russell with Dan O'Herlihy in The Travels of Jaimie McPheeters (1963).

36

Carroll O'Connor in ''The Green Opal Affair'' on The Man From U.N.C.L.E. (1964).

Type casting? As the egotistical actor Rocky Rhodes, Burt Reynolds offers unsolicited literary advice to William Shakespeare (John Williams) in ''The Bard'' on The Twilight Zone (1963).

Acting work of any kind was scarce for those brave souls who chose to stay in New York during the sixties. Robert Redford landed a supporting role in the prestigious *Producers' Showcase* presentation of "The Iceman Cometh," and stage actress Jean Stapleton won a small part in the film *Up the Down Staircase.* Others subsidized acting lessons and low-paying stage work with soaps and commercials well into the seventies. Ellen Burstyn, Armand Assante, Louise Lasser, and Kathleen Turner did time on *The Doctors;* Ted Danson, Sigourney Weaver, and Jo Beth Williams on *Somerset;* Roy Scheider, Robert De Niro, Dustin Hoffman, Morgan Fairchild, and Jill Clayburgh all did a stretch on *Search for Tomorrow.*

Dustin Hoffman supplemented stage and soap work on Search for Tomorrow by hawking the Volkswagen Beetle in television commercials (1965).

Ellen Burstyn in The Doctors (1964).

Jean Stapleton with Sandy Dennis and Robert Levine in Up the Down Staircase (1967).

Salome Jens and **Cliff Robertson** in "Man on the Mountaintop" on The United States Steel Hour.

37

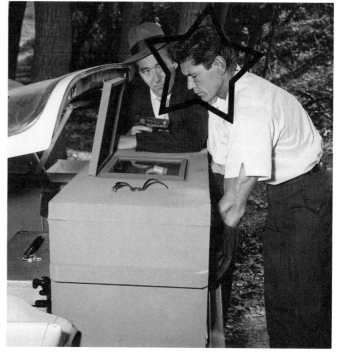

Leslie Nielsen's versatility led to an MGM contract and later, after many years of unsung supporting work, to legendary status as a comic lead in Airplane and The Naked Gun.

Here, searching through an attic full of memories, Leslie Nielsen stars in Playhouse Fifteen.

He'd put in time as a Native American (Apache) and tough guy (House of Wax, Machine Gun Kelly, etc.) before turning to television in 1958 for Man with a Camera. **Charles Bronson** left his special "car-trunk developer" behind after breaking through in The Magnificent Seven in 1960.

38

After making his New York stage debut with a walk-on in The Old Lady Says No! in 1948, **Darren McGavin** moved on to television, where he would star in no less than seven series.

She ended up just like she'd started—on television in high heels and hot pants. As a struggling starlet, **Angie Dickinson** paid the rent by being a Durante girl on The Jimmy Durante Show. (Angie's Number 18.)

Not everyone was lucky enough to work in prime-time television. Many young actors struggled through years of grueling work on the soaps—memorizing dozens of lines of dialogue nightly to be performed live the next day. Gena Rowlands did time in *The Way of the World;* Eva Marie Saint and Martin Sheen in *The Edge of Night;* Jack Lemmon and Patty Duke on *The Brighter Day;* Sandy Dennis and James Earl Jones in *The Guilding Light;* George Maharis, James Coco, Don Knotts, Hal Linden, and Lee Grant in *Search for Tomorrow.*

Efrem Zimbalist, Jr., played the handsome international lawyer Jim Gavin on <u>Concerning Miss Marlowe</u>.

39

Hal Holbrook used a melodramatic drunk scene from <u>The Brighter Day</u> as his audition for the Actors Studio.

The hosting chores on kids' shows usually went to weathermen or anyone around the station who didn't mind wearing clown paint or a funny nose. Very few of these unsung heroes went on to bigger things. Bob Keeshan, Ed McMahon, and Willard Scott were three exceptions.

Buffalo Bob Smith, Howdy Doody, and **Bob Keeshan** as Clarabell on The Howdy Doody Show (1950).

40

Although he stayed in children's programming, Bob Keeshan was miserable during his days on The Howdy Doody Show. Keeshan was given short shrift by Howdy's creators— particularly Buffalo Bob Smith, who regarded him as a no-talent who could be trusted with only the barest bits of on-screen funny business. Keeshan, for his part, considered Smith to be an egomaniac. But Keeshan proved to be a favorite with viewers and the decision to fire him in 1950 was quickly reversed when outraged viewers jammed NBC affiliate lines with their protests.

Once a stooge, always a . . . **Ed McMahon** stars on Big Top.

As a teenager, **Merv Griffin** played the organ and sang at weddings for $20. (Funerals were $5 extra.) His first professional TV work was on a local talk show in his native San Mateo, California. A hit record with the novelty tune ''I've Got a Lovely Bunch of Coconuts'' led to national TV exposure on the quiz show Play Your Hunch.

There was no such animal as a TV star when Lucy and Uncle Miltie first took to the screen a million years ago. (In fact, there were barely movie stars.) Television would ultimately rescue their careers, as well as those of countless other, lesser lights, whose personas never ignited on the screen. But first they were obliged to spend years as unsung supporting players in features or second leads in action B's and grade-Z horror flicks. The public indignities of such efforts knew no bounds: Robert Vaughn had to wear a loincloth as a Teenage Caveman and Clint Eastwood played back-up to a talking mule. But at least you could tell who they were. Michael Landon wore a fright wig and fangs as a Teenage Werewolf and James Arness was a giant carrot in *Them.*

Milton Berle in Poppin' the Cork (1927).

41

Lucille Ball in Kid Millions (1934).

Vivian Vance in The Secret Fury (1950).

Robert Blake and Humphrey Bogart in The Treasure of the Sierra Madre (1948).

Elinor Donahue and Margaret O'Brien in The Unfinished Dance (1947).

42

Raymond Burr, with John Ireland and Marsha Hunt, was a heavy in more ways than one in Raw Deal (1948).

Barbara Billingsley in The Unfinished Dance with Cyd Charisse (1947).

James Garner with William Holden in Toward the Unknown (1956).

Clint Eastwood officially dates his career from the role of Rowdy Yates on Rawhide, but he got his big break in a Francis the Talking Mule movie. That means that Clint and Francis (not to mention Mr. Ed) shared the same mentor—director Arthur Lubin.

Michael Landon with Dawn Richard in I Was a Teenage Werewolf (1957).

43

Clint Eastwood in Francis in the Navy (1955).

Larry Hagman and Brian Aherne in The Cavern (1965).

As a young actor, **Robert Vaughn** was subjected to the full-blown starlet-treatment at MGM. It took The Man From U.N.C.L.E. to overcome his loincloth period as a Teenage Caveman (1958).

The Unsinkable Joan

Although Joan Collins did deign to attend a studio charm school during her years as a starlet in London, she didn't bother much with acting classes. "I don't have to study," she informed her fellow students as she filed her nails. "I have a contract with Sir Arthur Rank."

I Believe in You (1952) was the first of nine films Collins would do for Rank before being brought to America to become Twentieth Century–Fox's "answer" to Elizabeth Taylor. At Fox, she did time in bosom-and-sand movies like *Land of the Pharaohs* while putting up with studio boss Darryl Zanuck's advances. ("I'm the biggest and the best," he informed her by way of introduction in a studio hallway. "You haven't had anyone till you've had me.")

When Collins' career as a hotbox bottomed out in the late sixties, she wound up doing appearances on British and American TV shows like *Star Trek*—sometimes with guest star billing, sometimes not. Reduced to American International cheapies like *Empire of the Ants* by the seventies, she gamely went through the motions with a fleet of tacky mechanical ants. In dire financial straits after her daughter suffered a serious brain injury after being hit by a car,

44

and as Twentieth Century–Fox's "answer" to Elizabeth Taylor in 1955.

Joan Collins in her first film for J. Arthur Rank, I Believe in You (1952) . . .

Collins returned to England in search of work. There, desperate for money, she hustled a lurid novel written by her little sister, Jackie, called *The Stud,* which was made into a sexploitation film featuring lots of skin (particularly Joan's). A similar Jackie-penned soft-core porno film called *The Bitch* followed. Both films were respectable box-office earners; but while they paid a few bills, they didn't exactly turn Joan's career around. She was doing the British equivalent of dinner theater when she got a call from Aaron Spelling offering her the part of Alexis on *Dynasty.* Reluctant to get involved in such an "iffy" series, she eventually signed on, against her better judgment, and the rest, as they say, is history—and *National Enquirer* headlines.

For young actors based in Hollywood, the idea was to do television until a screen break came along. Although some never made it in the movies, they became stars nonetheless.

John Forsythe was one of many aspiring screen actors who ended up as TV mainstays. Here he stars with Noreen Corcoran in "New Girl in His Life" on The General Electric Theatre (1957), the precursor to the beloved series Bachelor Father.

Newcomers **Warren Beatty** and Barbara Turner back up David Wayne in "Heartbeat" on Suspicion (1957).

45

Robert Duvall with Claire Griswold in "Miniature" on The Twilight Zone (1963).

Elizabeth Montgomery on The Untouchables (1960).

Although they started out on the stage and in movies, the three best known members of *Star Trek*'s stellar crew would rescue their careers by booking passage on the starship *Enterprise*.

Leonard Nimoy went from the title role in the antique boxing B Kid Monk Baroni (1952) to Zombies of the Stratosphere (a Republic serial) before slipping back into bit roles on Dragnet and Sea Hunt.

William Shatner distinguished himself on the Broadway stage in Joshua Logan's The World of Suzie Wong in 1958; but in the main he operated on the level of journeyman TV actor—always dependable, always bland—destined (if not for Star Trek) to a lifetime of "and special guest star . . ." roles.

Leonard Nimoy in Zombies of the Stratosphere (1952).

46

6034-1

De Forest Kelley had leading-man ambitions when he starred in Fear in the Night (1947) . . .

but his pretty-boy looks already had gone slack by the time he showed up in a 1954 episode of The Lone Ranger.

48

Toiling in the trenches of independent cheapies, newcomers like **Joan Van Ark** and Sam Elliott got slimed in movies with names like Frogs (shown here) and Barracuda.

Tyne Daly, with Don Stroud, as a hippie gal in Angel Unchained (1970).

As a Hammer girl, **Stephanie** (Sister Kate) **Beacham's** emoting provided the only entertaining moment in things like Inseminoid (aka Horror Planet, 1982).

Two of Hollywood's coolest blondes started out in lackluster TV series:

49

Michelle Pfeiffer as the ice-queen sorority girl of Delta House . . .

and **Kim Basinger** as a cop on Dog and Cat.

IT COULD BE YOU

As Ronald Reagan's final term in the White House was drawing to a close, the producers of *Dynasty* approached him with a $1 million offer to join the show in the role of one of Alexis's ex-husbands. *Dynasty*'s ratings were slipping badly, so the offer wasn't entirely frivolous. Ronnie was still one helluv'an actor —he'd proved that during Iran-Contra. Besides which, presidential precedent for such an appearance had already been set when Gerald and Betty Ford, along with former Secretary of State Henry Kissinger, played themselves on an earlier *Dynasty.*

But fundamentally, the producers looked to Reagan for the same reason voters did—the pleasure of his company. It is on the basis of such blatantly subjective factors that we choose our favorite TV actors. Sometimes we grow so attached to them that we let them hang around for years—regardless of whether they can carry a show. Certain TV personalities just keep turning up on one series after another, because they have a certain mysterious something that merits them a standing invitation into our living rooms. Finding an actor who has that particular X-factor is a casting director's Holy Grail—the single most crucial element in determining whether a new show flies.

Networks, studios, casting agents, and independent producers have routinely gauged that quality with the help of the "Performer Q"—a confidential tout sheet that rates TV performers solely on the basis of their likability. Every year the Q's creators, a small company in Port Washington, New York, supplies two thousand families with a list of 666 personalities and asks them, "Do you know this person?" and, on a scale of 1 to 5, "How much do you like him?" Over the years, the Q has become an indispensable tool for those behind the scenes—so much so that in 1987 the Screen Actors Guild charged that it constituted a form of blacklisting, one that apparently results in Ken Barry's being cast in every other new series.

Of course, it's not just a track record or a healthy TV Q that gets an actor noticed. Good looks, inside connections, a powerful agent, or a famous last name can also induce a casting agent to take your call. Actors armed only with talent are left to negotiate a heavily mined obstacle course consisting of the producer, the executive producer, the director, the casting agent, and the network execs, with only their talent to see them through.

On rare occasions—such as with producer Herbert Brodkin's inspired decision to go with the then little-known New York stage actors Michael Moriarty, Meryl Streep, and Rosemary Harris for the 1978 mini-series *Holocaust*—TV casting can be an enlightened adjunct of the creative process. But even with the class projects, the Big Events, it's usually the brand-name commodities who get the nod. Remember when Vera Miles was in practically every made-for-TV movie? Then it was Lee Remick, then Jaclyn Smith, then Jane Seymour. A variation on this take-no-chances casting strategy assigns a famous face to every role—from the leads to walk-ons—whether or not they're right for the part. And while it's always good to see former front-runners back in harness, an overload of old-timers and series-identified actors (also known as the *Love Boat* Syndrome) can be somewhat distracting—as when the Alex Haley family saga *Roots* brought together John Walton, Ben Cartwright, Lou Grant, and Morticia Addams!

Still, given all the built-in shortcomings of the casting system, it's amazing how often things go right, even if it's only by chance, not choice, that they do. No matter what the thought process (if it can be dignified with such a designation) that culminates in a particular actor's being cast in a particular role, some create a chemistry that allows them to inhabit their characters so naturally as to make the accidental seem inevitable. So you think the role of Perry Mason was conceived with Raymond Burr in mind, or Sheriff Matt Dillon created for James Arness? Well, wake up and smell the coffee crystals, baby. Those actors were fill-ins. Substitutes. Next-best-things.

As you consider the various casting vicissitudes that have shaped the shows you love, ask yourself if the grass would be as green, the sky as blue—if, indeed, you would be you—if Vivian Vance hadn't been Ethel Mertz, if Leonard Nimoy hadn't been Mr. Spock, and Jerry Mathers hadn't been the Beav.

Buffalo Bob and **Howdy** want you!

52

A frumpy, grumpy little man, decidedly lacking in either charm or warmth, William Frawley wasn't exactly in demand around Hollywood when he boldly called Lucille Ball and asked for the part of Fred Mertz on her new TV show. Though Ball had known Frawley for years, she wasn't at all sure he was right for the job. Frawley was sixty-four at the time and rumored to be an alcoholic. And then too, she had her heart set on Gale Gordon playing Fred. When it turned out that Gordon was committed to the role of Mr. Conklin on the radio version of *Our Miss Brooks,* Desi decided to give Frawley a chance to win him over. A long, wet lunch with Frawley left Desi convinced they had found their Fred. He managed to persuade Lucy easily enough, but CBS and the show's sponsor, Philip Morris, were a harder sell.

When Arnaz told Frawley that the honchos didn't think he could be trusted because of his affection for booze, he was furious: "Well, those bastards, those sonsabitches—they're always saying that about me! How the hell do they know, those bastards?" Desi, who wasn't exactly a teetotaler himself, didn't care whether Frawley drank or not, but because everything he and Lucy had was riding on the show, he knew that they couldn't afford any mistakes. "If you screw up," Desi warned him, "I'll not only fire you, but I'll have you blacklisted throughout the industry."

Lucy's dear friend Gale Gordon would eventually play Ricky's boss at the Tropicana on later shows, as well as her boss on *Here's Lucy* and *The Lucy Show.* As for Frawley, he remained completely professional throughout Lucy's run, never missing a day's work in all of its seven years—but, acording to Vivian Vance, that didn't keep him from spending most of his spare time in neighborhood bars.

Lucy wanted Bea Benaderet for the part of Ethel Mertz. But by the time *Lucy* was ready to cast, Bea had already begun playing Burns and Allen's next-door neighbor Blanche Morton. With their shooting deadline quickly approaching, director Marc Daniels dragged the Arnazes to a Connecticut summer theater to see Vivian Vance as the nasty sidekick in *The Voice of the Turtle.* Though Daniels had a tough time selling them on Vance, the real hard work began when it was time to sell Vance on playing Ethel. A

thespian of some standing (in her own mind, anyway), she was extremely reluctant to trade the roar of the greasepaint for the second-rate status of the small screen.

You'd have thought that the part of the lovable blue-collar lug Chester A. Riley (as in *The Life of*) would have been a perfect fit for Jackie Gleason, but his manic, bug-eyed delivery bombed with viewers, and the show was canceled after only one season (in 1949). Three years later, *Riley* was resurrected with William Bendix playing the part he had originated first on film, then in the radio series. An immediate hit, it stayed on the air for five years.

Having blown his big break, Gleason swore off TV—until two years later, when he was given the chance to host *Cavalcade of Stars,* a big-budget comedy-variety show broadcast over the now-defunct DuMont Television Network. It was there, of course, that he created the blue-collar lug of his—and our—dreams.

53

For the first three seasons of *The Honeymooners,* Alice Kramden was played by Pert Kelton, an actress known for essaying floozies and brassy, sassy wives. And Pert Kelton would have remained had she not suffered a coronary thrombosis while on the road with Gleason for a series of personal appearances in connection with the show.

Dozens of women had auditioned to take over the role when Gleason's agent, Bullets Durgom, decided to bring Audrey Meadows, then co-starring in *Top Banana,* up to Gleason's suite to meet him. Though perfectly civil to Meadows during the meeting, he jumped all over Durgom after she'd left. "Are you nuts?" he yelled. "That babe's way too young and pretty to play a middle-aged Irish housewife. Now quit wasting my time."

Upon hearing that she'd been rejected (and why), Meadows decided to employ some strategy to land the part: she had a photographer come over to shoot her one morning right after she'd gotten out of bed, in a house dress with no makeup. When Durgom

54

brought Gleason the photograph, he declared "That's our Alice. Who is she?"

Always loyal to old pals, Gleason brought Pert Kelton back as Alice's mother in the revamped *The Honeymooners.* "I didn't lose a daughter," she'd growl, gazing disgustedly at Gleason, "I gained a ton."

It was William Conrad's deep, resonant voice that gave life to the indomitable Sheriff Matt Dillon on radio's long-running hit *Gunsmoke,* but there was really no chance of his spinning with the show to TV. Short, stout, and balding, Conrad looked more like a counter man in a deli than the John Wayne type. Instead CBS opted for the genuine article by trying to sweet-talk John Wayne himself into taking the role with an offer of a hefty salary and a piece of the profits. But Wayne, correctly assuming that the public was still willing to shell out a few shekels to see him on the big screen, offered the producers a classic John Wayne type whom he himself had under contract—a young six-foot-seven actor named James Arness. Initially, the network was unimpressed since Arness's most impressive role at that point had been as a giant carrot in *Them.* Arness too was reluctant, but Wayne persevered. Wayne, by the way, received no compensation for his role in setting in motion one of the medium's longest-running shows. For over two decades, viewers would follow Arness's long legs down the dusty streets of Dodge City.

Alan Young was producer Arthur Lubin's first choice to play straight man to a wisecracking horse named Mr. Ed, but his original co-star was a horse of a different color. The Mr. Ed the world came to know and love was brought in after the dark horse (with no previous credits), who had originated the role in the pilot, was unceremoniously bounced from the series.

The last-minute cast change proved to be a fortuitous turn of events for the palomino who took over the role. A trooper, Mr. Ed did the show for six celebrated years and then toured the country making personal appearances at state fairs and supermarket openings until his death some fifteen years later.

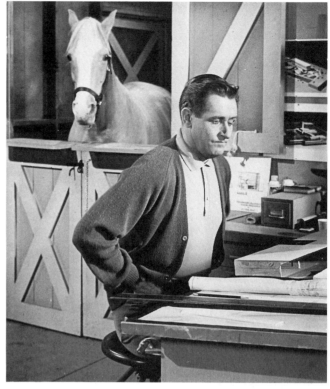

55

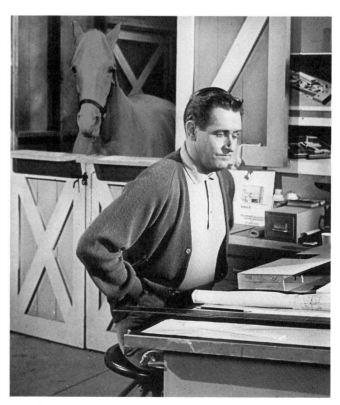

56

Fred MacMurray, the first choice for the lead in *Perry Mason,* turned down the role because he didn't want the work load of an hour-long weekly dramatic show. The part went instead to Raymond Burr, who had originally read for the supporting role of prosecuting D.A. Hamilton Burger. In landing the lead, Burr delivered himself from B heavies and *Godzilla* flicks, not to mention creating an indelible alter-ego that would dominate his entire career.

At forty-five, when most actresses of the glamour girl variety find themselves over the hill and out of work, Eva Gabor stumbled into her most identifiable (and lucrative) role ever on *Green Acres,* the *Petticoat Junction* spinoff. As the transplanted New York socialite Lisa Douglas, Gabor was, for a time, Hollywood's most popular TV actress. Here, finally, was the success that had eluded the Hungarian pastry for twenty years on the big screen. Oddly enough, though, the part had been intended for another actress, the beautiful Martha Hyer—an Academy Award nominee (for *Some Came Running*) who specialized in cold, unobtainable rich-girl roles.

Producer Paul Henning created the show for Hyer and Eddie Albert, but what he didn't count on was Hyer's expensive ($100,000 per appearance) price tag. Although the quality of her film offers would decline in the next few years, Hyer was still pulling down costarring roles in splashy film offerings (*The Carpetbaggers,* etc.) at the time Henning came calling. The producer subsequently tested twenty-six actresses for the part, finally settling on Eva. (Eva herself came perilously close to blowing her Hooterville gig by demanding that Henning employ her entourage of high-priced fashion slaves.) But Eva wasn't a shoo-in even then; CBS had strong reservations because her accent vas so thick, dahlink. Leave it to the brass to be the last to know that it would make the show.

If his wife hadn't gotten into the act, that perpetual boy-next-door Van Johnson would have become *The Untouchables'* tight-lipped enforcer with a tommy gun, Eliot Ness. The part had orginally been offered to Van Heflin but he turned it down, fearing it to be a mite too rough-and-tumble for a person of his stubby stature. Desilu's boss, Desi Arnaz, next approached Johnson, who agreed to a fee of $10,000 for the pilot ("The Scarface Mob"), which was to air in two hour-long installments on the *Desilu Playhouse.*

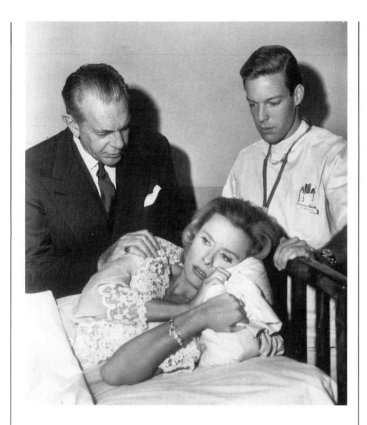

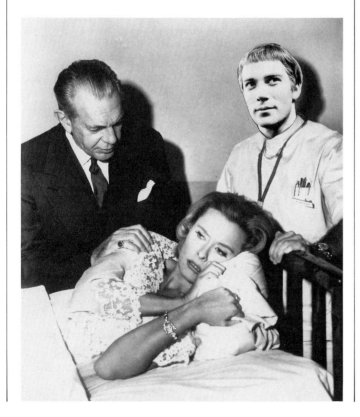

58

But on the Saturday night before the start of filming the following Monday, Evie Johnson, Van's wife and self-appointed agent-manager, called boss Desi and demanded twice that amount. "Either give him twenty thousand or he won't be there Monday morning." "Evie," Arnaz responded, "you know what you can do with Van, don't you?" (Van and Evie eventually split up. "She's gone," he said, when asked about her several years later, "and I hope she stays that way.")

Arnaz had taught the Johnsons a lesson, but now he was faced with paying off the dozens of extras and technicians booked for the shoot. In desperation, he thumbed through the *Academy Directory,* stopping short when he came to Robert Stack. It struck him that Stack had just the kind of WASPy looks and terse delivery to play straight man to brash ethnic underworld types.

Stack was reached at Chasen's restaurant in Hollywood at 2 A.M. on Sunday, but despite his agent's hard sell, he was dubious about the part. Independently wealthy from old California money, Stack couldn't be lured by bucks; and then too he was leery of long-term TV both because of the monotony and the fear that it would take the gloss off his big-screen career. Happily, Desi's smooth talk eventually won him over. On the case as Ness at 6 A.M. on Monday, Stack was greeted by a French wardrobe man who announced, "Meestaire Johnson, your clothes are ready."

Richard Chamberlain has William Shatner to thank for making him a star in *Dr. Kildare.* The white coat was passed to Chamberlain after Shatner declined the lead in order to play the earnest young district attorney in *For the People.* When that show turned out to be a dud, Shatner took the captain's seat on the Starship *Enterprise*—a spot that was originally to have been filled by film star Jeffrey Hunter, who had played the captain in the pilot. Hunter is said to have gotten cold feet about *Star Trek* after deciding it was really no more than an overblown kiddie show, but it's more likely that he was simply not available by the time the series was finally picked up by NBC.

As blasphemous as it sounds, the show, which suffered three humiliating cancellations during the course of its erratic run, might have fared better with Hunter in the role of Captain Kirk—initially, anyway. While Shatner was just an all-purpose utility man

known primarily for a number of standout shots on anthology shows like *The Twilight Zone* and *The Outer Limits,* Hunter was a big name star who might have won the show a little more respect, not with viewers, but with the networks.

Some actors lose out on a part by a nose. Danny Thomas nixed Mary Tyler Moore for the second incarnation of his older daughter on *The Danny Thomas Show* in favor of Penney Parker, because her "nose went the wrong way." (That's up instead of down.) But Mare's name came to Thomas's mind several years later when Carl Reiner and Sheldon Leonard happened to ask him if he could think of any *more* actresses to read for the part of Laura Petrie on *The Dick Van Dyke Show.*

In 1959, Carl Reiner took the wraps off his secret project, a pilot starring himself as Rob Petrie, head writer for a comedy variety show. It was called *Head of the Family* and, along with Reiner, featured Barbara Britton as Rob's wife and Morty Gunty and Sylvia Miles as Reiner's assistant writers on the show.

But although every network exec who saw it said it was great, Reiner couldn't seem to get one to commit to a deal. "I'm so angry. I don't know who to be angry with, but I'm angry," Reiner said. "Everyone agrees that I have a quality product, but nobody buys it." Something was wrong, and it took Sheldon Leonard to put his finger on it. "The show was great," he said to Reiner, "but *you* weren't."

The consensus was that Reiner was too ethnic and that the show might sell with a different, more white-bread cast. With amazing resilience, Reiner gave Leonard permission to "rewrap the package"; and after considering Johnny Carson and Dick Van Dyke, they finally settled on the latter after seeing him in *Bye Bye Birdie* on Broadway. Van Dyke solved the ethnic problem—although as the WASPy Rob Petrie he would nevertheless crack a lot of ethnic jokes (as when he observed that "April in Paris was nothing compared to spring at Grossinger's"). Reiner, of course, would end up playing boss Alan Brady to Van Dyke's Rob, who may have been TV's first sensitive guy, cute without being cloying, insecure, but secure enough to admit he had insecurities—a real middle-America-style mensch.

59

60

The role of the lovable but bumbling first mate of *Gilligan's Island* was offered first to Russ (*West Side Story*) Tamblyn and then to comedian Jerry Van Dyke (Dick's brother) both of whom took a pass. The William Morris Agency next recommended Bob Denver to *Gilligan*'s creator, Sherwood Schwartz. But because Denver had made such an indelible impression as Maynard G. Krebs, Schwartz couldn't imagine him as anything but a bearded, hip-talking freak. So a face-to-face meeting was arranged, and to his surprise and delight, Schwartz found Denver to be every bit as nerdy as the part of Gilligan required.

Having created a scintillating image as a soignée ghost in *High Spirits,* the Broadway musical version of Noel Coward's *Blithe Spirit,* Tammy Grimes must have seemed the logical first choice to play the earthbound witch Samantha on *Bewitched.* But Grimes infuriated the producer, William Dozier, by nixing the first script and demanding a rewrite.

While on the lookout for a less finicky soul, Dozier happened to get a call from his old friend Elizabeth Montgomery, who was trying to sell him on a sitcom property she wanted to do with her soon-to-be husband, director William Asher. Dozier turned down the script but managed to talk Montgomery into taking over for Grimes in *Bewitched*—even though she was five months pregnant at the time shooting began.

Tammy's fussiness is estimated to have cost her over $6 million in residuals.

Martial arts master Bruce Lee believed that he was born to play Caine, the karate-kicking Buddhist monk of the Zen western, *Kung Fu.* When the part went instead to round-eye David Carradine, Lee swore off Hollywood and decamped to Hong Kong, where he found his cult destiny as the king of ''chop sockey'' movies.

Many years later, he would be avenged by his son Brandon in the role of a hired killer engaged to assassinate Caine in the made-for-TV *Kung Fu: The Movie.* Unfortunately, the symmetry of that turn of events offered no solace to Lee; he'd died mysteriously in 1973 following a brain aneurysm (aggravated, it is suspected, by untreated wounds, epilepsy, and possibly anorexia).

61

62

It was David Janssen's smoldering charisma that made *The Fugitive* the big winner in its time slot from 1963 to 1967. And in turn *The Fugitive* made Janssen a big star—whose perks included a $4.5-million-a-year salary and his own custom-made trailer complete with library and a covey of attendants (one exclusively assigned to keeping him sober). But Janssen got the role of Richard Kimble only after dependable utility man Robert Lansing turned it down.

Although the pilot movie for *The Waltons* was *The Homecoming* (1971), author Earl Hamner, Jr., had first used its basic elements eight years earlier in the movie *Spencer's Mountain,* with Henry Fonda as the head of a large brood, a-lovin' and a-strugglin' and somehow gettin' by. Andrew Duggan played the paterfamilias in *The Homecoming* but was bypassed for the series in favor of Fonda. However, as much as he admired *The Homecoming* (far more than *Spencer's Mountain*), Fonda turned it down after astutely deducing that John Boy, not the father, had become the story's central character in the TV incarnation. Little-known stage actor Ralph Waite inherited the role of his life and played it for nine seasons.

If Gene Roddenberry's original vision for *Star Trek* had been realized, it would have been screen heavy Martin Landau rather than Leonard Nimoy who inflicted the Vulcan nerve pinch on Klingons and Romulans. Landau turned down Spock to play Rollin Hand, *Mission: Impossible*'s master of disguise—a role tailor-made for him by his friend producer Bruce Geller. Fearful that TV appearances would sully his reputation as a film actor, Landau "guest-starred" in twenty-six of *Mission*'s first twenty-eight episodes, then stayed on for three more years before quitting over a salary dispute. Nimoy, having just hung up his ears after *Star Trek*'s cancellation, once again followed in Landau's footsteps and signed on with the team at *Mission: Impossible.*

In one of his typically savvy career moves, Mickey Rooney nixed the meaty part of Archie Bunker on *All in the Family,* believing it and the show to be

63

64

far too rough for TV audiences. "If you go on the air with that crap," he admonished the show's producer Norman Lear, "they're going to kill you dead in the streets!"

Unlike Mickey, Penny Marshall was hot for the show; and, in fact, she came very close to being cast in the role of Archie's little girl, Gloria. But though she gave a sharp reading and was particularly effective in improv sessions with the already cast Rob Reiner, her real-life husband, Lear ultimately decided to go with Sally Struthers—rightly figuring that her vulnerability would make her a more pliable comedy foil to Archie than the hard-edged Marshall, and that her fair complexion and button-cute features were a more believable match with those of the very Irish Carroll O'Connor.

Sanford and Son wasn't always about a black father and son team. In fact, *Sanford and Son* wasn't even always about Sanford and Son. A Bud Yorkin import from England (like *All in the Family*), it had been called *Steptoe and Son* in its original incarnation. After two failed pilots, Yorkin bought the rights from Screen Gems and tried his own pilot, starring Barnard Hughes (later of *Doc*) and Paul Sorvino. When that pilot also bombed, and Yorkin decided to make the show black—an audacious move for the time, and one that might not have paid off so handsomely without the right lead. That lead appeared to Yorkin in the form of an X-rated comedian named Redd Foxx—who showed Yorkin he was more than just a dirty mouth in a small but hilarious part (of a crotchety junk dealer) in *Cotton Comes to Harlem.*

Bing Crosby as the wily, rumpled Columbo? It's true: And, in fact, Crosby, the producer's first choice for the lead in the TV show, was actually a reasonably close match to the man who had originated the role on the stage in *Prescription Murder:* Irish-American character actor Thomas Mitchell (Scarlett's dad in *Gone With the Wind*). But Crosby, who didn't exactly need the money, or the aggravation of a series grind, turned it down because it would have interfered with his real passion—golf.

66

Eventually, Peter Falk, whose twitchy street-kid style is about as far removed from Der Bingle's ba-ba-ba-boo mellowness as you can get, was recruited for the part. Falk, a (literally) cockeyed actor with a gravelly voice, would make Columbo one of TV's great characters. Relying on brains, not bullets, he scuttled sideways into his cases, a disheveled figure in an ancient, grimy raincoat, feigning incompetence to throw all the canny murderers off balance. "I was the tenth guy chosen," Falk recalls. "I don't know who the guys in the middle were, but it's interesting how, in about a month, your choice can go from a good-looking singer with a pipe to a one-eyed actor with a New York accent."

Anthony Andrews, the teddy-bear-clutching Sebastian of *Brideshead Revisited,* was the original pick to play that smooth sleuth Remington Steele. But Andrews was holding out for film roles and turned the part down. It was all for the best, really; for while he certainly filled the bill in the suave department, Andrews was far more believable playing the love interest to Jeremy Irons than he would have been to Stephanie Zimbalist.

Casting the lone-wolf avenger of *The Equalizer* presented a bit of a sticky wicket to the show's creator, Michael Sloan. "It was great to write this cool, compassionate, sophisticated guy. But who was going to play him?" The answer appeared in the form of Edward Woodward, a no-nonsense, somewhat unsung actor who'd toiled on the British stage and screen since the 1950s. But CBS, doubtful that Woodward's crisp Savile Row elegance would translate to American audiences, was dead set against the idea. In fact, if the network had had its way, it would have been Hollywood hipster James Coburn meting out justice on the mean streets of New York.

"Hip parents, square kids" was the original high-concept concept for NBC's *Family Ties.* Since the parents were to be the show's focus, there was no need to fret too much over casting the rest of the family.

So no one did. Much. Justine Bateman, a high school student with no real acting experience, was cast as the spacy older daughter, Mallory. Tina Yothers, a comer in the movie *Shoot the Moon,* was tapped to be the serious young Jennifer. And Matthew Broderick—a standout in *War Games*—was offered the part of Alex Keaton, the juvenile industrialist with a heart as big as the Federal Reserve Bank. But when it turned out that Broderick didn't want to leave the New York stage and Neil Simon, the part went instead to newcomer Michael J. Fox, despite the network's veto. "That's a face you'll never see on a lunchbox," sneered NBC programming whiz Brandon Tartikoff after getting his first look at Fox. Even the show's creator, Gary Goldberg, was unconvinced of Fox's charms at first. But the show's casting director, convinced that she had discovered a secret genius, persisted—ultimately convincing Goldberg to bet on Fox, at the risk of losing the show.

The cliff-hanger that concluded *Dynasty*'s first spring season ended with a heavily veiled mystery woman disrupting a courtroom scene during the murder trial of Blake Carrington. Not until the fall would viewers learn that she was none other than Blake's former wife, the glamorous and vengeful Alexis. Initially Alexis was to have been played by Sophia Loren or Raquel Welch, Sophia being the first choice. But Sophia nixed the part of the "female J.R." in the belief that her fans would never believe she could be so venal and manipulative and cruel. (And anyway, she was busy trying to sidestep serving a sentence for tax evasion in an Italian slammer at the time.) Instead of stooping to series TV, Sophia saved herself for statusy made-for-TV movies like *Brief Encounter* with Richard Burton and *Sophia Loren: Her Own Story,* thereby paving the way for Joan Collins to become the most celebrated British thespian to hit Hollywood since Olivier.

Television lore is full of all sorts of intriguing last-minute casting switches. *Dallas* was originally created as a starring vehicle for Linda Evans, for example, but when the part of Pam turned out to be peripheral, it went instead to former *Playboy* centerfold Victoria Principal. In fact, practically the entire population of Southfork traded identities at the last minute. Ken Kercheval was originally slated for the part of ranch foreman Ray Krebbs, and Steve Kanaly read for the part of Bobby Ewing. Kanaly wound up playing Krebbs, while Kercheval became J.R.'s archrival, Cliff Barnes. The part of the nefarious J.R. was seriously discussed with Robert Foxworth (who went on to star in *Falcon Crest*), and the role of Sue Ellen went to Linda Gray instead of the presumed front-runner Mary Frann (Bob Newhart's wife on *Newhart*). The show's producers probably didn't think any of the changes mattered since the actors were all unknowns. Of all the cast, only Patrick Duffy, who'd just jumped ship from *The Man from Atlantis,* was considered to have anything resembling marquee value.

69

Golden Girls creator Susan Harris had originally brought Bea Arthur, Rue McClanahan, and Betty White into the show to reprise characters they'd done so delightfully before: Arthur would be the caustic, Maude-like Dorothy; Betty White would be Blanche, a man-crazy Sue Ann Nivens type; and Rue McClanahan as the spacily saccharine Rose would play off her old role as Vivian, Maude's cheerfully vacant neighbor. But that was the last thing any of the women wanted to do; anxious to break out, all three coveted the role of Sophia, the wisecracking octogenarian. Director Jay Sandrich appeased his stars by having McClanahan and White read each other's roles during a rehearsal—which they did with such relish that the roles were officially switched on the spot. And Dorothy's edges were softened to make Bea Arthur happy, gently nudging her out of the Maude mode. Sophia went to Estelle Getty, the first

choice for the role from the minute she auditioned to the time the producers got around to hiring her several months later.

In landing the part of Maddie Hayes on *Moonlighting,* Cybill Shepherd surmounted the vigorous objections of the ABC brass, who saw her as being too brittle, too lacking in the kind of warmth that keeps viewers tuning into a series week after week. But while the show's creator Glenn Gordon Caron pooh-poohed Shepherd's Ice Queen image, describing her as sensitive and vulnerable, he also let slip the fact that the interplay between his male-female leads was to be an updating of *The Taming of the Shrew.* What he wanted from Cybill, whether he said so or not, was the very quality that had put off the network—the petulance so effectively exploited by Martin Scorsese and Elaine May in *Taxi Driver* and *The Heartbreak Kid,* respectively. Cybill would be feisty, and slick Tim Matheson would be adorable— the epitome of the new, sensitive male.

When it turned out that Matheson was otherwise engaged with movie work, the taming of this particular shrew was left to newcomer Bruce Willis—who won over Caron with his cocky cool, and the already cast Cybill by dropping his eyes downward at his first audition with her and murmuring demurely, ''I can't read with you . . . you're too beautiful.''

71

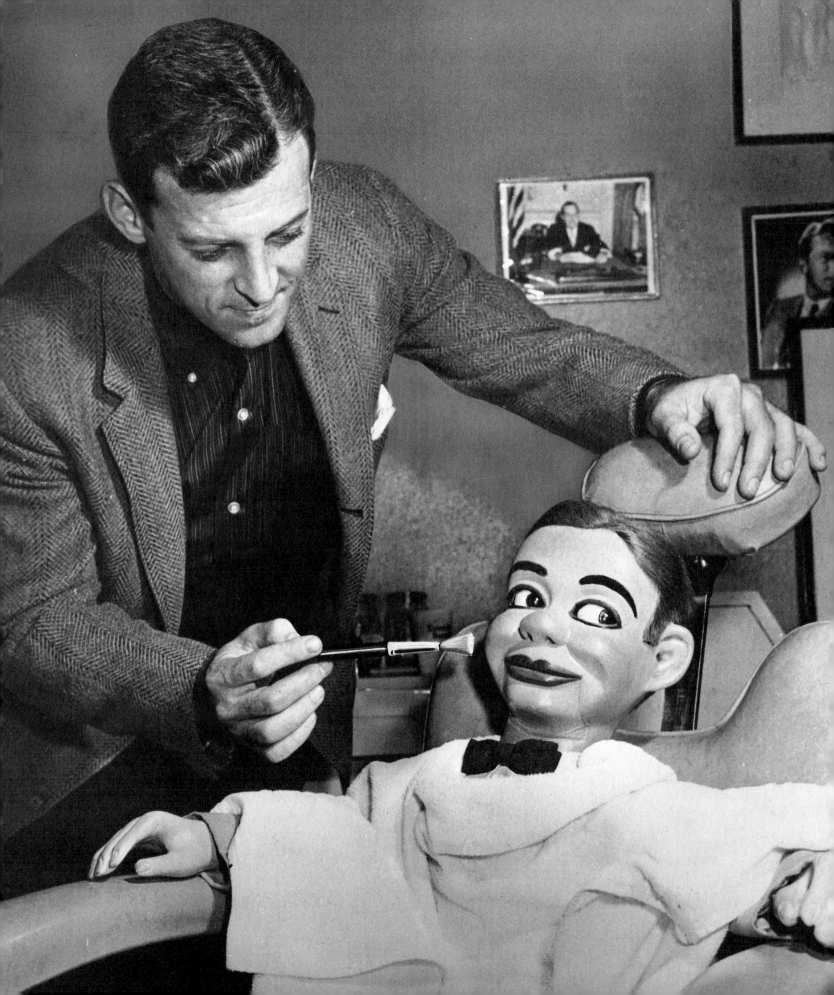

HOW DID THEY GET THAT WAY?

By their fluffy hair, glossy lips, and pearly-white capped teeth shall ye know them. They're so lithe, so lovely and pneumatic, they seem almost . . . well . . . "bionic." What brave new world is it that hath such creatures? The one in the box, of course.

You thought movie stars epitomized physical perfection? Well, think again, baby. There's nothing more boring than Christie Brinkley cover-girl flawlessness blown up to 70 millimeter projection. The big screen has always had a crush on quirky, irregular features that coalesce into one glorious, implausible whole. (Think Harlow, Bogart, and Dietrich.) It revels in the exotic, polishing it to a high sheen and making it even more idiosyncratic than it was to begin with—particularly now that movies have become so enamored of realism and "real faces." (Think Streep, Hoffman, and Whoopi Goldberg.) Television's scaled-down size, by contrast, is partial to perfection. What constitutes glamour on the small screen are those absolutely symmetrical features and "all-American" good looks that might elsewhere spell vacuity. Television then applies all the techniques and cheats originated by Hollywood to what is already flawless. Sure, sure, we know all about Roseanne Barr . . . but for every Roseanne there are a zillion Morgan Fairchilds. (And if they aren't that way to begin with, they will be by the time the reality adjustors have finished with them.) The glowing vision of Cybill Shepherd—meticulously coiffed, exactingly made up, and rendered through a shimmering halo of diffusion on *Moonlighting*—epitomizes television's propensity for gilding the lily, hiding blemishes that never existed, perfecting the perfect.

Of course, it wasn't always so. There was a time when the only star who looked good under the banks of broilingly hot lights required for live broadcasting was Howdy Doody. Early television's primitive photography—and cosmetology—techniques were particularly devastating to the stars of the studio era, who were accustomed to having their images lovingly rendered through flattering camera angles, filters, and lighting. They had faces then, all right; but

not necessarily the ones that were presented to the public. Stars like Bette Davis and Mary Astor, whose every film and 8-by-10 glossy had been meticulously retouched during the decades of their studio tenure, appeared to have metamorphosed into odd caricatures of themselves when they appeared on early television dramas. It's no wonder that stars who were still viable at the box office remained aloof from television, until technology and Max Factor could catch up to the fledgling medium's needs.

Stars who owned their own series were in a better position than most to make sure their carefully nurtured images were protected. Loretta Young brought a cadre of makeup and costume specialists with her from Paramount when she moved to television. And Lucille Ball lured veteran cinematographer Karl Freund out of retirement to make sure she looked as good in *I Love Lucy* as she had during her glory days at MGM.

Photography techniques began to catch up to those of the movies as more television production originated from the West Coast. If, for example, you look closely at reruns of old *Perry Mason* episodes, which were shot in Hollywood, you'll notice that their black-and-white texture is every bit as lush as that of any movie of the period, and that every cast member, from the stars on down to the most minor bit, has been painstakingly costumed, pancaked, and outfitted in store-bought hair (whether they needed it or not). In an aesthetic that harkened back to the theater, television's cosmetic artifice was not subtle. Indeed, it sometimes came right out and made its own editorial comment. The complicated system of clamps and pulleys that Eva Gabor wore under her wigs during her stint on *Green Acres*, for instance, were pulled so taut that hardly a trace of pesky emotion marred Eva's perfectly beautiful, masklike face.

Anatomy is destiny for a TV star. And TV star anatomy is some of the choicest in the world. Here then are a few words on how the stars got that way, how they stay that way, and how it's affected their destinies—and ours.

Paul Winchell preps his co-star **Jerry Mahoney** for a broadcast of their 1950 comedy-variety show.

Lucy as rendered by Engstead's older camera.

Faye et cleavage.

74

Lucille Ball came of cosmetic age in the thirties, a time when stars compensated for skimpy lips not with silicone or collagen injections but by painting an artificial bow outside the lips, regardless of their natural contour. The method produced an artful cheat on film and a bizarre clown mouth in real life. Ball continued to wear the look long after it had gone out of style. Her favorite photographer, John Engstead, who shot her first still portraits at MGM, and photographed her later when she was a TV star, remembers: "One of Lucy's trademarks, besides the mop of red hair, was that huge mouth that she painted on. I thought it was too big at one sitting, so I asked my assistant to cut it down just a trifle in all the black-and-white proofs. I was sure Lucy wouldn't notice, but when she saw the retouched proofs, she snarled: 'John, somebody has made my mouth smaller. You have to put my lips back.' "

As Lucy herself aged, she grew solicitous of Engstead's photographic equipment. "You'd better be a little more careful today. Your camera is getting older all the time."

TV's first glamour girl was Faye Emerson. At the time of her 1950 TV debut on her own talk show, she was best known as wife to Franklin Roosevelt's son Elliott and femme fatale in a string of minor roles at Warners. Her plunging necklines became her TV trademark—remarkable enough to have transfixed the elusive Marlon Brando during one of his rare television interviews.

Okay, Dagmar, you can take a breath now. . .

THE TITS THAT TOOK OVER TV: To a great extent, the legendary Dagmar was comedian Jerry Lester's creation. He'd hired the young unknown actress to do walk-ons on *Broadway Open House,* the first late-night talk show (1950–51). He then transformed her into a comedienne by having her recite bad poetry in a flat, deadpan voice. He'd even given her her name. And while Lester couldn't take credit for Dagmar's biggest claim to fame, he *was* responsible for making her chest—and her—a national joke.

Manic and aggressive, Lester hogged the action and called the shots, and yet it was Dagmar who became the sensation of *Broadway Open House.* By the second year of the show, she was pulling more publicity and almost as much money ($3,250 a week) as the star. Lester unsuccessfully tried to sabotage her by hiring another chesty blond (Barbara Nichols) to steal her thunder. But ultimately, Dagmar's chest would push him off his own show and out of television altogether, to be followed only too soon, alas, by Dagmar herself.

Puberty worked a stunning change on Walt Disney's prize cupcake, Annette Funicello. One day the sweet-faced, modestly talented Italian kid from Utica, New York, was just another moppet in the Mouseketeer lineup; the next, she practically formed her own row. Largely as a result of her stunning metamorphosis, she was catapulted from mouse to movie star.

At first the folks at Disney were blind to Annette's burgeoning potential; in fact, they were downright dismayed at the way she was growing up and out—until somebody noticed that her fan mail had escalated to an amazing one thousand letters a week, most of it, not surprisingly, from teenage boys. (It didn't hurt that an entire generation of baby boomers happened to be going through puberty along with Annette.) Finally recognizing her special talents, the Disney people plucked Annette from the Mouseke-ranks and gave her her own continuing series on the show. Several sappy feature films were also built around her, but none were particularly successful—primarily because Annette wore entirely too many clothes. It took the "Beach Party" movies to bring out her real talent.

Although we haven't seen nearly enough of Annette in the last few years, Johnny Carson can still get a laugh by describing something as being "bigger than Annette Funicello's training bra."

75

Annette and her pubescent Mouske-sisters.

Nothing in the ratings surveys of *Charlie's Angels* made specific mention of Farrah Fawcett's nipples, but her habit of running around sans underwear in every episode had everything to do with her overwhelming popularity, especially among male viewers. Farrah, the clear favorite right from the show's initial preview tests, capitalized on her popularity by posing for a poster that highlighted her best points.

Charlie's Angels begat a whole television genre called "jiggle TV," which reached its apotheosis during the reign of Suzanne Somers on *Three's Company.* Somers, too, released a pinup; but by then, fans had already seen far more of her in *Playboy* skin spreads taken during her earlier, leaner starlet years.

Suzanne doffs her brassiere and dons industrial grade nylon tights (under her jogging shorts!) to get her jiggle in the right places.

Though they may sometimes seem like vain creatures whose idea of fun is having liposuction, television stars, like movie stars before them, are required to stay forever young. Cosmetic surgery is but one of the sacrifices they make to maintain the fantasy of impervious perfection. So show a little compassion for someone like Katherine Helmond, whose face is so taut, she's beginning to look like she did in the movie *Brazil.* And how about a moment of silence for Totie Fields, who died of complications following a face lift?

"I cut off my nose to spite my race," Milton Berle informed his audiences after he had his nose "bobbed." "Now I'm a thing of beauty and a goy forever." Of course, not everyone chooses to be so candid about nose renovation. Dean Martin's nose job might have remained his secret if Jerry Lewis hadn't stood behind his back miming a nose being "cut" while Dino crooned romantic ballads. And while Joan Rivers has had her face, eyes, nose, stomach, and thighs recontoured (her first face lift was at age forty), she leaves the plastic surgery jokes to Phyllis Diller. "I've had so much plastic surgery," Diller likes to say, "that the only original parts left of me are my elbows."

As Maude, Bea Arthur was the first series character to undergo a face lift (although the real-life Bea didn't remodel herself till several years later). In 1984 Jeanne Cooper of *The Young and the Restless* went Maude one better by having her character (Kay Chancellor) undergo an actual facelift on camera, thereby allowing audiences to view the surgery in all its bloody reality and then follow her progress as she mended over the next few months.

Following her celebrated divorce from Peter Holm, Joan Collins wowed London by flashing a cleavage that appeared more pneumatic than usual. When the British scandal sheets speculated that Joan had augmented her already imposing bustline, she threatened to sue. Busy girl that she is, however, she never got around to taking the case to court.

One of the perks Eva Gabor insisted on when agreeing to take the starring role on *Green Acres* was bringing along the well-known makeup man Gene Hibbs. As the show went into production, Hibbs devised a mechanical (as opposed to surgical) face lift for Gabor based on a technique that had been used earlier for Lucille Ball and Barbara Stanwyck.

The procedure began with the affixing of several discreet adhesive patches to the top of Eva's forehead and above the ears. Tiny silver hooks embedded in the tape were attached to elastic cords which encircled her scalp and were hidden under the elaborate bouffants and wigs she wore as Lisa Douglas. With the bands pulled tight, Eva's face remained supernaturally taut—even when she got allergic smelling hay.

The contraption was so crucial to Eva's *Green Acres* allure that she refused to give Hibbs a two-day leave of absence to do the makeup on Judy Garland's corpse—even though Liza Minelli had made a special request. Although it must have seemed heartless at the time, it's easy to understand why now: Who would have cranked Eva's face?

During the run of *McMillan and Wife,* one of the show's cameramen put pressure on Rock Hudson to have a tuck taken in his eyelids. Hudson finally acquiesced, but only grudgingly, since he couldn't see the need. He remained happily convinced of the perfection of his looks well into his late fifties, although heavy drinking had left him with a pronounced paunch and sagging skin. Even after his dramatic deterioration from AIDS, he saw only his finer points as he watched himself on *Dynasty* each week—frequently exclaiming to friends, "I think I look good, don't you? I look the way I did when I first started acting."

THE MOUNT RUSHMORE AWARD: In 1983 Carol Burnett underwent oral surgery to correct an acute overbite and the "buck teeth and receding chin" that had given her a lifelong "ugly duckling complex" not to mention twenty-five years of self-deprecating comedy material.

77

"The reason I came off being sexy and attractive —I still can't bring myself to say 'pretty'—is because I have had myself rebuilt. I had the hair under my arms taken care of. And I had an operation to firm up my breasts. And I spend about a thousand dollars a week to have my toenails, fingernails, eyebrows, and hair put in top shape. I'm the female equivalent of a counterfeit twenty-dollar bill. Half of what you see is a pretty good reproduction, and the rest is a fraud."

Modesty . . . thy name is Cher.

The truth is that even with acne, a blobby nose, and crooked teeth, Cher was always delicious. And now, thanks to a number of well-chosen improvements (in addition to all that hard work she professes to in her Jack LaLanne ads), she's more perfect than a retouched *Playboy* centerfold. The first high-profile baby boom star to recontour her face and body, Cher's a living monument to plastic surgery, the first truly Bionic Woman—as *Mirabella* recently christened her.

Cher's cosmetic overhaul began in 1977 after the cancellation of the new *Sonny and Cher Show* (and the birth of her son, Elijah Blue Allman), when she had her breasts lifted and firmed. She went on to have the same operation two more times—presumably until her beleaguered breasts couldn't get any firmer or higher. But it wasn't until she saw herself in 35-millimeter magnification on the big screen that she began to remodel her face. Boom! The newly renovated serious-actress-model Cher had a contoured nose, higher cheekbones, straight teeth, and unconfirmed rumors of other improvements as well.

Danny Thomas has gotten a lot of mileage out of his oversized nose ("My nose is so big," he likes to say, "I can vacuum lint off the carpet from a standing position"); but if studio boss L. B. Mayer had gotten his way, Danny's trademark beak would have been downsized to more petite proportions. Mayer urged Thomas to have surgery when he first arrived in Hollywood in the mid 1940s saying, "People expect to see pretty things, beautiful women, handsome men on the screen." Thomas did not agree. "The world is composed of not-so-beautiful people," he told Mayer, "and besides, I would be ashamed to go home to my eight brothers if I did that."

This noble stand may have limited Danny at Metro, but he believes it helped make him on TV: "People rooted for me, the ugly man, to keep that beautiful wife," he said.

(Danny's daughter, Marlo, wasn't nearly so principled. But who can blame her? Danny's nose looked even worse on her than on him.)

Marlo Thomas (right) with her father, **Danny**, mother, **Rose**, and sister, **Terry**, circa 1955.

A NOSE BY ANY OTHER NAME UPDATE: Dinah Shore, Gracie Allen, Nanette Fabray, Milton Berle, Perry Como, Dean Martin, Jerry Lewis, Bobby Van, Edie Adams, Zsa Zsa Gabor, Eva Gabor, Barbara Eden, Marlo Thomas, Lee Majors, Stefanie Powers, Sonny Bono, Cher, Joan Rivers, Phyllis Diller, Victoria Principal, Katherine Helmond, Barbara Barrie, Joan Van Ark, Connie Sellecca, Lisa Hartman, Michele Lee, Melanie Mayron, Barbara Bosson, Deborah Raffin.

THE NO-NOSE NANETTE AWARD: Rue McClanahan

TV hair policy is sometimes dictated directly from the top—as with the decision to let *The Price Is Right*'s emcee Bob Barker's hair go gracefully gray. "The executives at CBS—from Bud Grant right on down—checked it out," said Barker, who had sportingly allowed the network hairdressers to experiment with several interesting interim shades. "After it turned blue, then red, I finally decided the patriotic thing to do was to let it go white." Fortunately for Barker, the network brass agreed.

They're not always so amenable, however. Producers practically wrestled Walter Winchell's hat off his head when he made the move from radio to television. "It's not polite to wear a hat on TV," they told him. "It's my trademark!" the columnist howled. "And besides, Judy Garland wears a hat on TV." Winchell eventually capitulated, thus exposing to the public for the first time his nearly bald head.

If Walter Winchell was the first TV personality to attempt to wear his hat like a toupee, Carl Reiner was the first to wear his toupee like a hat. After being a slave to his hairpiece for several years on *Your Show of Shows,* Reiner began going without it while creating *The Dick Van Dyke Show.* But that was behind the scenes. He didn't go public until the episode in which he had Laura Petrie blurt out on national TV that Rob's boss, Alan Brady—played by Reiner—wore a toupee. From that point on, Reiner became casual to the point of hilarity about his hairpiece—wearing it one night on *Johnny Carson* and then going without it the next morning on *Today.*

Walter Winchell

79

Carl Reiner

William Shatner, 1958

1966

1984

Stacy Keach

Millions of viewers discovered that Howard Cosell wore a toupee after Muhammad Ali playfully plucked it off during a *Wide World of Sports* interview. Until then, audiences didn't particularly think of TV stars or broadcasters as wearing toupees, although when you check out some of the golden oldies—early *Perry Mason*s, for example, in which every male player, from the leads to the walk-ons, was outfitted with flagrantly fake hair—you wonder how we failed to notice.

A few of TV's new breed—Gerald McRaney, for one—display their chrome domes with pride. Even old-timer Pernell Roberts ditched the rug he wore on *Bonanza* when he became Trapper John, M.D. And character actors like William Conrad, Ed Asner, and Danny DeVito are allowed to go au naturel. And yet the Hollywood tradition of disguising a retreating hairline by whatever means necessary is still honored by most of television's leading men—where, luckily for them, it's easier to get away with the cheat than on the big screen.

Today's TV-star toupees run the gamut from the cunningly sparse "balding" patches worn by Bruce Willis and *Doctor, Doctor*'s Matt (*Max Headroom*) Frewer to Charlton Heston's bushy thatch, which

Larry Hagman, 1959

1978

1989

Pee Wee Herman

looks like it escaped from a department store dummy. What all those little pelts of store-bought hair have in common, though, is that they are just as closely guarded a secret today as they ever were—this in an era when virtually every other aspect of a star's life is public.

The time has come, however, to rip off those rugs and let the light of day shine down on those gleaming pates. So here's a rundown of some more TV stars—past and present—who are less than the sum of their parts.

Jack Benny, George Burns, Fred MacMurray, Macdonald Carey, Bing Crosby, E. G. Marshall, Don Porter, Lloyd Nolan, Andy Williams, Jack Paar, Carl Betz, Jack Edwards, Ralph Edwards, Jack Bailey, Gale Gordon, Steve Allen, Don Knotts, Lorne Greene, George Maharis, William Shatner, Martin Landau, Darren McGavin, Jack Klugman, Michael Ansara, Ricardo Montalban, Edward Woodward, Gil Gerard, Willard Scott, Burt Reynolds, Stacy Keach, Harry Anderson, Robert Mandan, Steve Martin, and Joe Penny.

IF IT'S NOT A TOUPEE, IT SHOULD BE DEPARTMENT: Ted Danson

IF IT'S NOT A TOUPEE, WHAT IS IT? DEPARTMENT: Bruce Willis

81

Burt hanging on to his own hair in <u>Hawk</u> . . .

. . . and newly coiffed in a spiffy salt-and-pepper number for <u>BL Stryker.</u>

82

As a young actor on *Hawk,* Burt Reynolds shaded in his bald spots with eyebrow pencil, eventually moving on to other elaborate camouflage, including a Zero Mostel–ish comb-over. He was wearing a sporty salt-and-pepper number (as well as a new, un-lined face) when he returned to TV in 1989 as *BL Stryker.*

Like Carl Reiner, *Today* show weatherman Willard Scott makes no attempt to hide the fact that he wears a toupee, even going so far as to doff it to the camera when the spirit moves him. An earlier *Today* show host, Hugh Downs, also went public with his hair loss, regularly monitoring his transplant surgery (at the time a revolutionary new procedure) for the edification of his viewers.

There must be something about turning auteur that gives a guy the courage to dispense with his rug, since Rob Reiner, like his father before him, has foresworn his Meathead hairpiece now that he's a big-deal director. And Tony Randall doffed his piece when he went legit on Broadway in *M. Butterfly.*

WHAT—AND GIVE UP SHOW BUSINESS? DEPARTMENT: While *Night Court*'s Harry Anderson is never seen on the bench without his hat or a hairpiece, co-star Richard Moll goes the opposite route and shaves his head for the role of Bull. It seems Moll auditioned for the part shortly after doing a sci-fi movie, and the show's producers liked his mutant look so much they insisted he keep it.

Those elaborate hairdos you see Joan Collins wearing on *Dynasty* reruns are almost always wigs. She's got a million of 'em—each one so lifelike that almost nobody, including her directors, realizes it's not the real thing. (By the way, although her friend Zsa Zsa Gabor says Joan is bald, it's more likely that she's just lazy.)

THE FARRAH FAWCETT-MAJORS LOOK

THE CUT

Farrah Fawcett's famous look starts with a layered haircut on long hair. Starting at the top and holding hair straight up, cut to the desired length (about 3 inches). Using this length as a guide, pull each section of hair straight up, measure to the cut strands, and snip off. Hair is almost at a 90-degree angle when cut.

Except for the time she dyed it blond as a surprise for Rob, Laura Petrie's brunet flip-styled helmet never varied by a hair, thanks to the industrial-strength lacquer used by the *Dick Van Dyke Show* hairdressers. "There was so much spray on my hair," Mary once said, "you could hang clothes on it."

Here it is, folks—the flip that will live in infamy: the famous lacquered blacker-than-black hair hat worn by Marlo Thomas as *That Girl*'s Anne Marie looked like it could deflect small-caliber bullets at close range.

83

America's crush on Farrah Fawcett may have cooled since her heady Angel days, but the leonine coif she affected while on the show lives on in the hearts and on the heads of the girls at the mall and the bowling alley.

The Farrah flip was achieved by taking a round brush, wrapping freshly shampooed and gelled hair around it counterclockwise, and training a blazing-hot hair dryer on it until it started to sizzle. "Frosted" bleach-blond hair enhanced the desired wire-mesh texture, and a layer of lacquer cemented it in place.

THE SET

Set section of hair across the top in three big pincurls (or vary the style by using rollers).

The crown, back, and nape area rollers are all going down.

THE COMB-OUT

Although George Reeves was in excellent shape during his years as the star of *Superman,* his body had to be padded with slabs of sponge and rubber in order for him to make the transition to the Man of Steel. These foam rubber "muscles" were sewn into a cut-off tee-shirt, to keep them from moving around under his Superman leotard. Co-star Jack (Jimmy Olsen) Larson fondly remembers Reeves making everyone on the set giggle by "mincing around in his tights and cape."

On various episodes of Loretta Young's TV anthology show, the star's breasts, buttocks, calves, and thighs were padded. Lovely Loretta was also the first to commission (from the designer Irene Sharaff) an upholstered body stocking with an artificial latex neck to reproportion her shoulders and long swanlike neck. Loretta is said to have held on to the contraption for years, despite its deterioration and gamey smell—much to the chagrin of costume people who dressed her.

Upon meeting James Garner for their first scene together in the new western *Maverick,* Jack Kelly looked the lumbering six-foot-three actor up and down and then whispered in his ear, "Would you do me a favor and stand in that fucking hole before you start talking?" And though his studio bio said he was five foot ten, Bob Conrad wore three-inch heels for his role in *The Wild, Wild West,* and the CBS casting office had orders not to hire any women over five six. No similar limitation was placed on male players, but the producers saw to it that he never played a scene in which he was surrounded by tall (i.e., over five six) men.

DO NOT ADJUST YOUR TV: Delta Burke was knee high to a caterpillar when Ann Sothern first began wowing TV audiences with bizarre weight fluctuations. Sothern had been just a little wisp of a thing when she played Maisie during the forties, but her weight ballooned wildly during her years as Susie McNamara on *Private Secretary.* To distract viewers' attention up toward her fabulous face, she wore elaborate collars and bodice decorations. Yards of tulle petticoats were added to her circular skirts—so many, in fact, that she ended up looking like a Rose Bowl float. During those periods when even tentlike coats couldn't hide her extreme avoirdupois, Sothern delivered all her lines while sitting at her desk. On the

84

Can you find Superman's muscles?

Loretta with her recontoured neck.

rare occasions when she stood, she practically hid behind the file cabinets.

But no matter what her weight, she was still a photographer's dream. As John Engstead observed: "Fat or thin, she was an excellent subject. She put on careful makeup with expert shadings. When she knew I was ready to shoot, an amazing transformation took place. She would pull her head up from her shoulders by stretching her neck, so that the cheeks would go in a trifle, the eyebrows were raised, and there was that Sothern face, a face that gave no clue that it is attached to a large body."

Most of us took Jackie Gleason's bulk to be part of his comic persona. And it is true that Gleason had been overweight almost all his life. But Archie Mayo, who directed him in *Orchestra Wives* (1942) for Fox, thought he was good looking enough to become more than just a comic stooge, that is, if he'd just take off some weight. Excited by what he saw as his big break, Gleason shed fifty pounds—only to have Mayo decide that he wasn't funny thin. Frustrated (and famished), Gleason returned to New York, television and a good hot meal: three steaks and four or five shots of bourbon (his usual).

WHAT OPRAH TOLD DELTA THAT SHE WOULDN'T TELL ROSEANNE DEPARTMENT: In 1988 Oprah Winfrey lost enough weight (150 pounds) to create another talk show host. She credited the loss to a liquid diet and "fear of tabloids," which had milked her bulk for years in screaming headlines that had it causing her to lose her job, her man, and her mind. Also supposedly listed as in jeopardy of being fired from their respective series if they didn't slim down were Kirstie Alley, Roseanne Barr, Don Johnson (during *Vice*'s 1986–87 season), and Delta Burke —who ballooned to two hundred pounds during the third season of *Designing Women.* Of course, the stars' fat-fighting problems were not nearly so interesting to the networks as they were to the tabloids, which saw in them a story with which a great many supermarket shoppers could identify.

TELL THAT TO CHARLES KURALT DEPARTMENT: In 1983, Linda Ellerbee was informed by NBC higher-ups that she would have to lose weight if she expected ever again to anchor at NBC News. Ellerbee didn't lose weight, and she didn't anchor the news. And so it goes.

Connect the dots: Susie McNamara during one of her zoftig periods.

85

Jackie Gleason in <u>Orchestra Wives</u> (1942).

PETTICOAT JUNCTION

Loretta Young, the First Lady of Television in the fifties, made the Ten Best Dressed list three times during her show's eight-year run. "I believe that wearing the correct dress for any occasion is a simple case of good manners," she proclaimed. And Loretta was nothing if not well-mannered. The extravagant gowns she wore as she made her sweeping entrance on her weekly show were the epitome of chic for millions of viewers (and, like Dinah Shore's yards of chiffon, the object of a great deal of good-natured satire). Loretta understood that you are what you wear. Although reduced to the mostly inelegant milieu of television production, she nevertheless managed to bring with her the extravagant studio approach to fashion. But she and Dinah were the exceptions. During television's early days, fashion played the most minor of roles. Most wardrobes came from a costume rental house or an actor's closet—particularly on live shows that emanated from New York, as opposed to those filmed in Los Angeles. In those days, a show's entire fashion budget would just about cover the cost for one of Joan Collins's *Dynasty* whatsits. And one show, *Cameo Theater,* cut even that figure in half by limiting camera movement to close-ups that showed the players only from the waist up.

Seventh Avenue got an idea of the impact television could have on the marketplace when *I Love Lucy* struck lucrative merchandising tie-in deals with several clothing manufacturers to produce popular ready-to-wear items like Lucy Lingerie and Desi Denims. (Could you die?) The overwhelming public response to these products was not lost on television's powers-that-be. As they came to realize what a lure fashion could be in terms of attracting viewers, special looks were created for its series regulars. Over the years fashion has become more and more important to the overall look and appeal of television shows, gradually evolving to its current exalted status as a star in its own right. Today television acts as a veritable fashion gazette of the air, an influential disseminator of trends that range from era-defining looks like *Dynasty* glitz to subtle hipsterisms like Karem "Duane Wayne" Hardison's flipped-up Cazel shades.

But however much or little attention is paid to television fashion, the clothes we see on the small screen provide a kind of semiotic signpost of their time. The bugle-beaded extravaganzas of the prime time soaps reflected and reinforced the Reagan era's obsession with opulence, just as the modest shirt-waists worn by the Happy Homemakers of the fifties were an expression of that era's homespun values. The preceding decade had seen women in slacks and no-nonsense suits. But those spunky go-getting gals who populated wartime-era films had been recast for television as proper wives and mommies by a post-war propaganda campaign designed to nudge women out of the work force and back to the kitchen. True, fifties fashion was a pretty drab affair to begin with, but it became even more so as interpreted by television. TV wives and moms (as conceived by male writers and producers) were dressed with all the elan of civilian nuns, in the spirit of the nonsexual, brownie-making machines they were meant to be. Though provocatively attired bombshells like Monroe and Mansfield still roamed the big screen, they were apparently too racy for home use—except late at night when Dagmar snuck out on *Broadway Open House.* During peak family viewing time, women were ladies and they had the demure duds to prove it. It took Mary Tyler Moore in her Laura Petrie capri pants to challenge the taboos and help women slip into something more comfortable.

Beginning in the sixties, television didn't just reflect, or interpret, the way people looked; it became an acknowledged influence on fashion. The sweater-clad Andy Williams helped to loosen up the stiff, buttoned-up style of the 1950s. The mod look, minis, Pucci prints, and psychedelia all got a push from the bimbos on *Laugh-In.* Figure-baring, body-hugging disco fashion got a boost from Cher on *The Sonny and Cher Goodtime Hour.* And in addition to their drop-dead gowns and slinky street clothes, *Charlie's Angels* popularized sweat suits, tennis shoes, and T-shirts for everyday wear and made brassieres obsolete. The Angels had an average eight costume changes per episode (a whopping twelve for Farrah when she made a guest appearance in 1979). "Men looked at the girls," the show's designer Nolan Miller

Loretta sez: "Wearing the correct dress for any occasion is a matter of good manners."

rightly observed, "and the women looked at the clothes." And they bought them too. That the show's influence continues to flourish is borne out by Jacqueline Smith's enduring status as a beauty guru with her own highly successful line of K-Mart fashions.

Female fashion on television became a virtual caricature of itself with the campy creations worn by the sirens of *Dynasty.* Nolan Miller's oversized shoulders recontoured the female silhouette into something resembling a linebacker in drag. (But women didn't care so long as their hips looked smaller.) *Dynasty* also had an effect on menswear, particularly on those little upscale necessities like cashmere scarves and leather attache cases that make life bearable. But it was *Miami Vice* that jolted men out of their sartorial doldrums. The decked-out detectives Crockett and Tubbs provided men's fashion with a social and moral object lesson: Good guys wore Armani and bad guys wore polyester. Suddenly, it was acceptable for red-blooded men to wear pink and go without socks. By the end of *Vice's* second blockbuster season, retailers were reporting a significant rise in the number of sports coats purchased by men and a decrease in the sale of conventional suits.

Fashion's impact has been more than just a matter of trendsetting; it has influenced social mores by reinforcing clichéd stereotypes. It's even changed the course of television history . . . sort of. Dissatisfaction with drab, out-of-date dresses contributed to Vivian Vance's malaise on *I Love Lucy* and drove Jan Clayton from *Lassie!*

But as far as you and I are concerned, the question of how fashion has affected TV is much less interesting than how TV has affected fashions—particularly the ones we wear.

Here are a few of the silly things it's made us do . . .

Millions of women chortled at the sight of June Cleaver and Harriet Nelson doing housework in tailored dresses, high heels, and the ever-present strand of pearls. (A sitcom mom was demure while asleep as well; CBS censors required *Father Knows Best's* Jane Wyatt to wear a brassiere even under her flannel nightgowns.)

Harriet in her housewife drag.

In contrast to Loretta Young's fashion-cum-etiquette statement, the guiding spirit behind Lucy Ricardo's wardrobe was Lucille Ball's belief that it should not be more extravagant than the income of a modestly paid nightclub entertainer would allow. Much less glitzy and glamorous than her big-screen box-shouldered drag, Lucy's TV look tended toward shirtwaists with huge bows and polka dots, topped off with silly little hats. She wore the same outfits repeatedly, and on the occasions when she did don swanky clothes or showgirlish costumes (to pull of some sort of Lucy Ricardo–style mischief), it was explained that she had rented them from an agency. (Apparently, that same agency had a factory outlet on Gilligan's Island, given the limitless changes of costume available to the shipwreck victims.)

Lucy's hausfrau wardrobe was so convincing that millions of women jumped at the chance to imitate it. Anxious to cash in on *Lucy's* tremendous popularity, dozens of manufacturers around the country struck

88

merchandising tie-in deals with Desilu, and by the show's third season, three thousand retail outlets carried collections of Lucille Ball dresses, sweaters, and blouses. Desi too became a trendsetter for the masses, reviving the vogue for smoking jackets and lending his name to the first line of star-endorsed jeans, Desi Denims. Other Lucy merchandise included Lucy Lingerie, costume jewelry, and a whole array of baby products that attempted to capitalize on the birth of Little Ricky. But the biggest *Lucy* fashion hit was the matching he-and-she pajamas the Arnazes were contractually obligated to wear whenever they were in the vicinity of their he-and-she twin beds.

Desi and Lucy sell pajamas.

Before *Dynasty*, before Krystle and Alexis, there was Eva Gabor as Lisa Douglas, the farm-bound sophisticate of *Green Acres.* Only she could match Loretta Young's extravagance when it came to her TV wardrobe. Jean Louis, one of the greatest of Hollywood's costume designers (known for his glitzy wardrobes for Ross Hunter's big-screen soapers, was paid handsomely to make sure Gabor looked dazzling in the barnyard. Often she would have as many as seven costume changes during a half-hour show. But the expense turned out to be well worthwhile: the public adored the program's old-style glamour. Said Gabor, "In one episode I appeared in a Jean Louis gown I had worn just a few weeks earlier. Hundreds of fans wrote me asking, 'Can't you afford a new dress?' "

It was Mary Tyler Moore's idea to wear slacks on *The Dick Van Dyke Show.* "I suggested to Carl [Reiner] that when I vacuum the rug, I wear pants," she says. "I couldn't imagine putting on a little dress for that."

Laura Petrie's "capri pants" were skin-tight and ended an awkward six inches above the ankle, as if they'd shrunk in the wash. But while they were wildy unflattering to almost anyone but Mare, they became —thanks to her—a national fad. In the spring of 1965, *Time* magazine reported: "Mary Tyler Moore has helped make capri pants the biggest trend in U.S. casual attire."

However, a survey taken in the second year of the show saying that most women couldn't identify with pants convinced the show's producers to put Moore back in a dress—which she did "gritting my teeth." The ban lasted about three months. Then the show started getting letters saying, "Wait a minute! We liked her better in pants. Put them back!" A subsequent compromise allowed Mary to wear slacks in one scene per show.

90

Even at the height of his popularity on *Love That Bob,* Bob Cummings looked hopelessly dated as the photo-snapping sitcom swinger Bob Collins. In his role as a young bachelor, the mid-fortyish Cummings dressed in slim-fitting sports clothes, open-collared shirts, and more mascara than the starlets he chased through every episode. Still, his California casual wear—coming as it did during the era of the Man in the Gray Flannel Suit—made a substantial contribution to what has been called the "peacock revolution" and the overall relaxation of American male fashion.

Whadda hunk! **Bob** puts the make on **Anna Maria Alberghetti**.

With his sleepy eyes and pouty smile, Ricky Nelson (above) was a flesh-and-blood teenager, not a synthesized TV version of the real thing. (In fact, he was so real and so sexy that if he hadn't been the son of Ozzie and Harriet Nelson, he would probably never have been cast in the part.) While working his way toward teen-idol status on the show, Ricky wore his own raucous threads—disseminating the cool-cat look to millions of suburban teenagers.

Speaking of real teenagers, there were more than a few of those to be seen on *American Bandstand* during the fifties. They were the epitome of cool—those tough Italian kids from South Philly with names like Frannie and Sal. And the clothes they wore became all the rage with their white-bread audience, even though the fashion fads they spread—lace collars, sweater sets, rolled socks, and saddle shoes with a teeny-tiny belt in the back—were, in reality, spunky flourishes devised to jazz up somber Catholic-school uniforms.

Andy Williams (right, with Jonathan Winters) had a Kennedy casualness that was perfect for television. Slightly smaller than life, he fit perfectly into the box in the living room, and he dressed accordingly in a bland style that matched the decor of any home. He helped to move mohair cardigans and Lacoste shirts from the golf course into the realm of acceptable informal menswear by wearing them every week on his musical-variety show.

As the so-adorable-you-could-throw-up Buffy on *Family Affair,* the late Anissa Jones (left, with Johnnie Whitaker) was forced to wear frilly little dresses with puffed sleeves and sashes throughout the show's five-year run. The producers insisted that the cutesy-poo outfits were essential to Buffy's cuddly allure. And besides, her mother had signed her to a contract with a children's clothing manufacturer that paid them a handsome fee as long as she wore their line on the air. Anissa was still wearing what she bitterly complained were ''baby clothes'' at the age of thirteen, when *Family Affair* finally went off the air.

91

It wasn't dumb enough that Patty Duke had to play her own ''identical cousin'' on *The Patty Duke Show;* she was also forced to wear clothes that made her look like a geek throughout what was already a very public and painful adolescence. As the Scottish Cathy (who ''loves a minuet, the Ballet Russe, and crepes suzette''), she wore conservative dresses and separates, which, though drab, she preferred to the boxy things she had to wear as the American Patty (who ''loves to rock-'n'-roll; a hot dog makes her lose control''). Her Patty clothes seemed to her to be ''stiff and unreal—an extension of the trick photography and my trick accent. Nothing of it had anything to do with the way a human being of that age really moves or thinks or chooses clothing.

''Not only did I hate those clothes,'' she said many years later, ''but they put my name on some and successfully merchandised them, so a lot of other poor girls were walking around with the same ugly clothes I had to wear.''

There was no explanation offered for it, either thematically or aesthetically; but as Rhoda Morgenstern, Valerie Harper almost always wore some sort of gypsyish-looking shmatte tied around her head, particularly after she moved from *The Mary Tyler Moore Show* to her own starrer. The look has long been popular among both male and female bohos and self-styled working-class heroes. But Rhoda's head wraps appeared to have been more of a predilection of the actress who played her than a political statement on the part of the character (although Rhoda did have artistic pretensions of a sort—she was a window-dresser, remember?). Whatever the reason, the look caught on for a time with other artistically inclined working girls.

Happy Days used the 1950s as a benign cultural backdrop upon which to create gentle comedy, but its spin-off *Laverne and Shirley* blew up the look and sensibility of the era to cartoon proportions. Taking a cue from the caricatured costumes of the long-running Broadway musical (and later hit movie) *Grease,* the show lampooned fifties fashion to a fare-thee-well with poodle skirts, beaded sweaters, high-top sneakers, and motorcycle jackets, not to mention Squiggy's Bill Haley kiss-curl and the huge initial L's that adorned every piece of Laverne's wardrobe (including her pajamas). An integral part of the show's look and the source of many visual jokes, the show's campy clothes were instrumental in setting in motion the fifties style revival that swept the eighties—an era that had more in common with the conservative fifties than just poodle skirts.

Like another famous TV dad, Ozzie Nelson, Bill Cosby has made the sweater a basic—but this time around it's not just for at-home wear, and it's not just any old sweater. In order to keep pace with Dr. Cosby, it's got to be one of those pricey Italian numbers with an elaborate design and a label with a name like Versace or Missoni. These sweaters are so statusy now that they've become acceptable office wear for "creative" types. In fact, the look is common enough out in Hollywood that TV and movie execs, who used to be known as "the Suits," are now referred to as "the Sweaters."

93

Consider the genealogy of the Hawaiian shirt: it started out as corny tourist wear (usually accompanied by a lei and Bermuda shorts). A decade later, in an ironic twist, it became thrift-shop hip, a cheap-to-chic fashion statement. And then in the eighties, along came *Magnum, P.I.* to put an end—and a beginning—to all that. The trendy became a trend when hunky Tom Selleck made the Hawaiian shirt square again.

94

What was the fashion match of the 1980s? Why, Linda Evans and shoulder pads, naturally. Together with her *Dynasty* co-star, Joan Collins, Evans launched a bugle-beaded revolution in women's fashion that dominated the decade.

But Evans might never have been mated with shoulder pads if not for *Dynasty*'s costume designer Nolan Miller. And Miller might never have been mated with *Dynasty* (or *The Mod Squad* or *Charlie's Angels,* for that matter) if not for his chance meeting with an out-of-work actor named Aaron Spelling in a flower shop some thirty years ago. Of such accidents of fate, history is made.

It wasn't until *Dynasty*'s second season that the show became the fashion focal point of the universe. But that had as much to do with the political climate in the country as with *Dynasty*'s innate style. With the Reagans in residence on Pennsylvania Avenue, it was suddenly acceptable to take the diamonds out of the vault and resurrect the sables from storage. No one

typified this newfound love affair with ostentation more than *Dynasty*'s glamorous bad girl, Alexis—a paean to overstatement if there ever was one.

"Wardrobe is a subtle way of fleshing out a character," observed Miller. "With Joan Collins, I tried for a bold, hard edge that visually said, 'I'm a bitch.' " Collins in full Alexis drag revived a kind of fashion whimsy that hadn't been seen since Joan Crawford turned in her ankle-strap pumps. And, in fact, Miller had based Collins's early wardrobe on Crawford's haute bitch look. "I outfitted Alexis in Miss Crawford's style," he acknowledged. "I did fitted suits with peplums and big hats and furs. A very studied kind of look."

As that too-good-to-be-true angel of goodness, Krystal Carrington, Linda Evans was dressed in pastel colors and soft fabrics, but that didn't mean she didn't have her share of outlandish get-ups. "The idea was to dress characters the way people think the rich dress," Miller said. The image of the rich that Miller gave viewers was the one they saw in the society pages: jet setters and Euro-trash in lavish formal wear at big ticket benefits and Nancy Reagan in her borrowed Galanos.

Dynasty's high-flown sartorial conceits begat a slew of gussied-up imitators: Morgan Fairchild on *Paper Dolls,* Dina Merrill in *Hot Pursuit.* Even the Women of *Dallas,* who had made it a point to buy their clothes at local Dallas boutiques for authenticity's sake, bowed to *Dynasty*-inspired opulence and hired their own designer to come up with ritzy new outfits to wear around Southfork.

As far as the retail clothing market was concerned, the show's impact was mostly on women's fashions. However, the luxurious flourishes like the exotic leather attaches, designer tuxedos, and cashmere scarves affected by the Carrington-Colby clan caught on among men.

The rage for sequins and bugle beads may have fizzled along with the public's fascination with the life-styles of the selfish and shallow, but the oversized shoulder popularized by Miller's *Dynasty* vixens, while scaled down a bit, continues to live on.

Theirs was a world of lowlifes and scuzzballs who shot at them with Uzis and AK-47s. But oh, what clothes they got to wear while they were slumming. The flawlessly groomed Rico Tubbs was almost always nattily turned-out in a suit and tie, diamond stud in his ear. More casual, although every bit as resplendent, the perpetually tanned Sonny Crockett affected unconstructed linen jackets, baggy pants, sleeveless tees in peaches and pinks, expensive loafers (without socks) and Armani jackets no honest detective could afford—especially one who took home $450 a week.

But hey pal, Crockett and Tubbs couldn't exactly go around in standard cop issue if they were going to infiltrate the world of Miami's dope millionaires. And besides, their fancy threads were all confiscated. "Hell, even the shoes aren't mine," Sonny liked to say. Fortunately, most of the arrested felons in Miami had sensational taste and were just Crockett and Tubbs's sizes.

Miami Vice kicked off a revolutionary movement in menswear, softening fabrics and silhouettes. Suddenly it was okay for red-blooded males to dress up and to wear pastel colors usually reserved for new-born babes. But *Vice*'s style impact wasn't restricted simply to clothes; it also resonated in the upscale toys—the sports cars and speedboats and various high-tech gadgets like cordless phones—flaunted by both the good and bad guys.

Vice's stunningly innovative visual style changed not only the look of television, but that of Miami itself. During the show's early years, sets had been built to obtain the kind of interiors the production designers wanted. Gradually, they were able to do more location shooting as Miami began trying to copy the idealized version of the city the show created. Thirties-style touches, like glass bricks, ceiling fans, and Bauhaus curves, began reappearing in new buildings. And the quirky little Art Deco hotels of seedy South Beach, where much of the filming was done, took on new coats of pastel pink, green, and blue hues. Life began to imitate *Miami Vice* as Sonny Crockett look-alikes (many with Latin and European accents) dressed in pastel tee-shirts and espadrilles began showing up at cocktail parties and hangouts of the suddenly stylish South Beach.

TOO CLOSE FOR COMFORT

You're old enough to know the truth now. Ricky didn't love Lucy forever. Laverne wasn't exactly wild about Shirley. And Wilbur despised Mr. Ed. Sure, it hurts. But you've got to face facts: just because a TV team clicks in front of the cameras, it doesn't necessarily mean they want to hang out together in their custom Winnebagos. Ask Cybill and Bruce.

You might say that for actors, making a movie is like having a love affair, while doing a TV series is something like being married. A movie set is a fantasy kingdom where actors come together to perform a brief pas de deux. When passions flare between co-stars, as they so often do, they're usually of the amorous variety. However, you don't hear much about love blossoming on the sets of long-running TV series, now do you? Sure, it happens on occasion—as with James Arness and Amanda Blake on *Gunsmoke,* Meredith Baxter and David Birney on the (mercifully) short-lived *Bridget Loves Bernie,* Mia Farrow and Ryan O'Neal on *Peyton Place,* Michael J. Fox and Tracy Pollan on *Family Ties,* and Delta Burke and Gerald McRaney on *Designing Women.* But, as a rule, TV-star love affairs are usually between the stars and themselves.

Not that TV stars are more, shall we say, high strung than their film counterparts. It's just that the grueling pressures of the TV grind affect people very differently than the short-lived and inspired chaos of moviemaking. Series co-stars are in for the long haul; they're bound together until death or low ratings do them part. It's hard to say which is worse for a TV actor's mental health: a bomb that fizzles in a few weeks or a hit that hangs on season after season, ensnaring its hapless cast in a seemingly endless nightmare of work and ego-clashes, not to mention the thankless task of trying to top themselves week after week. It is any wonder that series stars are constantly at each other's throats?

Forget team spirit. Forget chemistry. The very nature of serial television dictates that no matter how chummy they may appear on screen, the great majority of series co-stars will find themselves locked in a battle for supremacy, with everyone fighting to be first in the hearts of the fans. That's what ignited the fireworks between *The A Team*'s George Peppard and Mr. T. Ditto Cindy Williams and Penny Marshall on *Laverne and Shirley* and the Not Ready for Prime Time Players on *Saturday Night Live.* Their rivalries were a simple matter of survival, of battling for a fair share of scripted shtick.

When we the public get wind of these wars, however, ratings may plummet, especially if it's crucial that we believe in the characters as friends or lovers to enjoy the show. Given the nudgy nature of Felix and Oscar's relationship, for example, it didn't particularly matter when we found out that the Odd Couple didn't hang out together in real life, but it was deadly for *Laverne and Shirley*'s ratings when their fans discovered that the two best-best-best friends had ended up on opposing sides in a nasty legal battle.

For many of us, one of the earliest TV traumas was being confronted with the terrible news that Lucille Ball and her husband, Ricky Ri . . . er, Desi Arnaz —had called it quits. How could that be? We'd been with them every week, and we'd never noticed anything was wrong. Oh, sure, Lucy blew up the kitchen every so often or got a loving cup stuck on her head, but Desi forgave her; in fact, he secretly loved her for it—didn't he?

The carefully maintained shroud of secrecy that surrounded the real-life hostility between the Arnazes during *Lucy*'s run was a holdover from the studio era, when any and all flaws were airbrushed out of the picture of the blissfully happy star with the blissfully happy life. And, of course, keeping up appearances was good business for Lucy and Desi. They understood that their standing invitation into America's living rooms depended on the communal fantasy of them as a loving couple.

Today, we know lots more about stars than we used to. Their off-screen bickering always seems to reach our ears, thanks to an "informed source" happy to blab everything to the *Enquirer* or the *Star.* As a result, scoring the behind-the-scenes battles has become a national pastime. But being the fickle creatures we are, we soon grow bored, and move on to other titillations, or other channels.

'No, really . . . we're the best of friends.'' **Ted Danson** and **Shelley Long** enjoy a romantic interlude on Cheers.

On rare occasions, off-screen fireworks can make certain kinds of on-screen action crackle—as with *Cheers*'s sparring lovers Sam (Ted Danson) and Diane (Shelley Long). There was competition between the two co-stars right from the beginning but the situation worsened when Long was tapped to star in several movies. One of them, *Outrageous Fortune*, became a runaway hit while Danson's screen career refused to ignite. But don't get the wrong idea. It wasn't simply that Ted and Shelley were competitive or that they didn't get along. No, it was worse than that: They just plain couldn't stand each other. And viewers knew it since their skirmishes were avidly chronicled by both the tabloid and mainstream press. But, as luck would have it, the tension between them dovetailed neatly into the scripted tension between Sam and Diane. In fact it made it more fun.

Separating fact from fiction keeps an army of tabloid tattles gainfully employed and a nation of confirmed voyeurs pleasurably engaged. Which is reassuring, in a way, since it would be a stone drag to think that there was no more to a television viewer's pleasure than simply what meets the eye. (Well, wouldn't it?)

Look at it this way—you've seen every *I Love Lucy* at least four hundred times. Now you're ready for the advanced class—for the kind of impertinent information you won't find in your *TV Guide.*

So, with that in mind, we give you the lowdown on TV's four-star family feuds. . . .

"I loved Dean almost as much as my wife and kids," Jerry Lewis once said of his ex-partner, Dean Martin. "I worked twenty-four hours a day to keep him liking me. I'd do crazy things like snipping off people's ties or gluing their shoes to the ceiling. But he was never as warm and outgoing as I hoped he'd be."

Hard as it must have been to resist such adorable antics, Dean Martin managed to remain oblivious to Jerry's charms during their ten-year partnership. In fact, the only way he could bear working with him was to slip away whenever possible or to ignore him altogether—no mean feat!

Dean was also a mite too glib for Jerry's tastes—particularly since Jerry was supposed to be The Funny One, the nerdy but lovable dimwit (sort of an Eisenhower-era Pee-wee Herman), with Dean ever the sardonic straight man. Norman Lear, who wrote for the team during their much-heralded five-year stint on *The Colgate Comedy Hour*, remembers,

"Jerry was bugged by how naturally funny Dean was. He . . . couldn't stand it if Dean got any laughs. Whenever [he did], strange physical things would happen to [Jerry] and he would wind up in a corner on the floor someplace with a bellyache. Sometimes he would go to the extreme of calling his California doctor to fly to New York and treat him."

To compensate for Dean's smart mouth, Lewis began horning in on the show's writing and producing chores. While Dean would do his usual cursory run-through of his lines and make for the chicks in the back booth at Hansen's Drug Store, Jerry put in long hours polishing their bits—that is, *his* part of their bits. Bud Yorkin, who took over direction of the show, remembers: "Very often Dean would ad-lib an exceptionally funny line at Monday's rehearsal and everybody would fall on the floor. We wouldn't hear it again until Jerry ad-libbed it on the air before Dean got the chance, so he'd be the one to get screams from the audience." Dean allowed Jerry to get away with murder, seemingly content to saunter through their routines, ever the straight-faced straight man—until the day in 1956 when he finally blew: "You can talk all you want about love," he told Jerry. "To me, you're just a dollar sign."

Relations between Dean and Jerry were further strained by the fact that their wives absolutely detested each other. Still, the duo might have lasted longer if they had stuck to movies rather than the high-pressure grind of TV. As it was, their partnership lasted a decade; their celebrated enmity for each other, lots longer. "When I feud with someone," Jerry said, "I don't forget, they don't forget, and history doesn't forget."

The two maintained their silence until twenty years after their breakup, when the one man who could make the impossible happen brought them together during Jerry's annual Labor Day Muscular Dystrophy telethon. "I have a friend backstage who wants to say hello," Frank Sinatra said coyly to Lewis on the air, and out walked Dean. After the show Lewis wrote Martin a letter and had it delivered to his hotel. There was no reply. Weeks passed and Lewis sent another letter, this time enclosing a twenty-dollar gold piece with his telethon symbol engraved on one side and a so-called "love inscription" on the other. Still no response. The following August, Lewis called Martin in Las Vegas to invite him back on the telethon. Dean sent word that he would meet Jerry at the Sahara at four o'clock. "I'm still waiting," Jerry says.

When it became fact and not just gossip-column prattle that Dean Martin and Jerry Lewis were breaking up in 1956, comedian Lou Costello took out sanctimonious full-page ads in the show-biz trades, saying the comics owed it to their fans to patch up

their partnership. "Sacrifice your egos," he wrote, "as Bud and I have learned to sacrifice ours."

But almost before the ink was dry on the *Hollywood Reporter,* Abbott and Costello, who had shared the primary hosting honors on *The Colgate Comedy Hour* with Martin and Lewis for several years, had a bitter fight of their own that resulted in Costello storming off the *Comedy Hour* to become a regular on Steve Allen's weekly TV variety show. Abbott, ailing from the shock of the split, checked into a hospital.

Nobody was more lovable on camera than Lou Costello, but off-screen he was the classic melancholy clown—a depressed man who drank heavily to ease the pain of the death of his adopted son in a drowning accident. Costello was also particularly bitter at having "carried" his partner for years. The late Mel Blanc, who worked with the duo on *The Abbott and Costello Show,* once recalled, "They hated each other. Especially Costello. Even at the end he was still trying to get other straight men, but he could just never find one as good." Costello was suing Abbott for $222,000 in unpaid royalties at the time of his death from a heart attack in 1959.

They were both television stars based in New York who often made the same Damon Runyon–esque beat, but there was never any love lost between Milton Berle and Jackie Gleason. Their animosity dated back to a particular night in the mid-thirties, when Berle discovered the chubby upstart doing a warmed-over version of his act in a little Mafioso club in Newark. Gleason would ultimately move from stand-up to acting, distinguishing himself as a comedy sketch performer; but for a time it seemed that whatever Berle did—clubs, burlesque, the occasional movie bit part—Gleason was always just a few steps behind him.

At first their rivalry consisted of a few barbs in the columns and some noisy exchanges at the Copa or Ciro's; but by the time (1952) that both were doing hour-long comedy variety shows on different networks, it had escalated into an all-out war for ratings and big-name acts. Gleason struck the fatal blow in 1954 by stealing Berle's longtime sponsor, the Buick car company. Berle got the news in his morning *Variety* on the way to work.

Once Buick had given Berle the boot, Gleason suddenly decided to phase out his comedy variety format (replacing it with a thirty-minute sitcom, *The*

Honeymooners), leading some to suspect that he'd hung on just long enough to kill off Berle. One person who thought so was Berle himself, who said, "Jackie made me what I am today—unemployed."

Cod-eyed, cement-faced, and so scaredy-cat-stiff he could barely unravel his vowels ("So letchearit forem") or pull off a simple introduction ("I'd like to *prevent* Robert Merrill"), Ed Sullivan lives in our memories as a man profoundly ill at ease in his role as a television personality. But out of view of the camera's unblinking eye, Sullivan was a steel-balled power freak; a savvy scrapper with a genuine eye for talent, combined with a killer competitive instinct that was ultimately responsible for exterminating a nest of viperish rivals—including Jack Paar, Arthur Godfrey, and Hedda Hopper.

Sullivan even subdued the lowest of the low, Walter Winchell—the columnist who had shattered once and forever the concept of privacy for public figures, the man who took credit for "inventing the low blow."

During their years as rival gossip columnists for two New York tabloids, Winchell and Sullivan divided the city's stars and their PR minions into opposing camps. But while Sullivan was influential, it was Winchell who ruled the roost—reaching almost 90% of the adult U.S. population with his daily column during the 1930s—and who, with his penchant for smear tactics and Red bashing, generated real fear among show-biz types and pols.

Winchell grew even more powerful upon moving into radio, where he became an immediate star reaching 21 million people with his Sunday night broadcast. But Sullivan upped the ante by jumping into TV. As his show picked up steam, he became more vocal in his dislike of Winchell, finally ripping into his rival on a New York radio show. Labeling him a character assassin, a blackmailer, and a power-mad menace, he then moved on to trace Winchell's career —starting with his days as a second-rate vaudeville hoofer—in unflattering detail. Winchell fought back, calling Sullivan a copycat and a fraud. He even intimated in interviews that the reason "Mr. Sunday Night" looked so stiff was because he had "the big C"—cancer.

At the height of the animosities Winchell launched his own version of Sullivan's weekly variety TV offering; but after a strong start, *The Walter Winchell Show* took a sudden nosedive. The problem wasn't a lack of pacing or of stars, it was Winchell

himself—with his rat-a-tat delivery and his grim unease in front of the camera, he made Sullivan look like cool incarnate. All viewers could see, as Winchell's biographer Michael Herr has written, was "an angry old guy with his hat on, yelling at the camera."

Seeing the tyrant falter, Sullivan began to accelerate his attack. He was abetted by an unlikely ally, Jack Paar, who, though he'd toadied mightily to the columnist during his early years, dismissed Winchell as a "has-been" and a "heel" on his own late night show. "What worries me is the hole in his soul," he sneered of his onetime booster. "His orchids are poison ivy in a crackpot. This type of guy wears the American flag like a bathrobe."

Smelling victory, Sullivan administered the coup de grace by presenting Winchell with a copy of a secret document he had somehow managed to unearth —the contents of which were so damaging that Winchell chose never again to tangle with Sullivan, either on TV or off. Without so much as a peep, he limped off the air after only thirteen weeks. Winchell's defeat marked the beginning of the end of his power to make and break careers, and the devastating loss of his popularity in print and radio.

The Winchell-Sullivan feud wasn't the only TV battle between titan tattlers. In an effort to imitate Sullivan's *Toast of the Town,* Hedda Hopper decided to move her radio series, *Hedda Hopper's Hollywood,* to TV. Hopper bullied superstars like Joan Crawford, Gary Cooper, Lucille Ball, and Bette Davis into making noncompensated appearances on her first special by suggesting that an itsy-bitsy nugget of naughty gossip just might make its way into her column if they didn't. As a result, Hedda not only got the same biggies as Sullivan but she got them first, and she got them practically for nothing.

Hedda's foray into TV posed a formidable threat to Sullivan—for a time, anyway. Sullivan managed to close down her show before it had a chance to get going by getting the TV actors' union to force her to pay her guests competitive wages.

Having made quick work of Winchell and Hedda, Sullivan moved on to diddle NBC's late-night upstart, Jack Paar. He started by blackballing acts who appeared on Paar's show for scale. Spewing moral outrage, Paar challenged Sullivan to a public debate. When Sullivan—who had nothing to gain from such a skirmish—declined, he found that he'd been made to look like the loser, especially to Paar's late-night constituency, who'd been whipped into an anti-Sulli-van frenzy by Paar's histrionics. But eventually Jack Benny took the wind out of Paar's overinflated sails by suggesting that his moral fervor was misplaced. "If you're gonna be mad at someone," he chided Paar one night on the air, "be mad at Eichmann or some-body, not Ed Sullivan!"

Despite this much-publicized feud, Paar was, to Sullivan, no more than a pest. He had a bigger prob-lem right on his home turf in the person of the "Old Redhead," Arthur Godfrey, with whom he was con-stantly vying for top-rung status at CBS. Paar was a genre unto himself, but Sullivan and Godfrey had a great deal in common—too much, in fact. Both were hosts of nighttime variety shows; both prided them-selves on their ability to discover and foster new talent; and both went in heavily for a spare, non-show-bizzy approach. ("That folksy shit of God-frey's," Sullivan liked to say, "just hides the fact that he's downright ignorant.")

But as it turned out, Sullivan didn't have to worry about either Paar or Godfrey. Both men's volatile na-tures would cause them to self-destruct in two sepa-rate and very showy on-the-air temper tantrums, thereby leaving Sullivan virtually unchallenged for twenty-three years.

Lucy and Desi were America's favorite couple in the fifties; but, ironically, *I Love Lucy* had been cooked up in 1950 as a way of keeping the two of them together. (Ball had sued Desi for divorce earlier, alleging he was "screwing everybody in sight.") Said Lucy: "It was either work together or good-bye mar-riage." And in a way, *Lucy* did keep the marriage afloat, but that didn't keep the specter of divorce from looming over the show.

Burdened by passionate love and hate, the Lucy-Desi union was too hot not to cool down. In truth, the marriage had been over for years before Lucy won a no-fault divorce from the California courts in 1960. Arnaz said, "The more we fought, the less sex we had, the more seeking of others, the more jealousy, the more separations, the more drinking. Add to this the herculean effort we had to make to maintain the imaginary bliss of Lucy and Ricky, and our lives be-came a nightmare."

Unlike her dizzy sitcom persona, the real-life Lucy was plenty tough. During her years as the boss and star attraction of the Desilu empire, she was a work-aholic—a "control freak 24 hours a day" as her

daughter, Lucy, later put it, and often abrasive in her zeal to achieve the top stardom that had been denied her during her years at RKO and MGM. "Lucy was mercurial," says one of the show's publicists. "She'd call you a son of a bitch one minute and come over and kiss you the next."

Every bit as driven as his wife, Desi Arnaz was the powerhouse who'd parlayed his and Lucy's $5,000 savings into millions in just four years. He overworked even when he played golf. Though Desi's intensity was offset by an innate warmth and gener-osity toward the people he worked with, he was a classic Hollywood-style womanizer and boozer, who seemed to regard his extracurricular activities as part of the rewards of being a Latin and a star. Desi, as one admiring woman friend put it, "could rumba standing up and lying down."

Arnaz juggled a suicidal work schedule with doz-ens of affairs, boarding his favorite mistresses on his yacht, the *Balboa,* while his family was neatly tucked away in Beverly Hills. As the stress of producing *Lucy,* and later godfathering *December Bride, Make Room for Daddy, The Untouchables, Mission Impossible,* and *Star Trek* among others, escalated, Arnaz began to drink heavily. At first, liquor had a galvanizing effect on him—sending him into intense bursts of activity that exhausted his staff. His constant carousing was quite naturally hard on Ball. "It was embarrassing," she said many years later, "the drinking, and the rest of it." Embarrassing—and becoming increasingly public—enough so that she gave up trying to keep the situation under wraps: On one angry occasion, Lucy locked Desi out of the house, forcing him to sleep in the lobby of the Beverly Hills Hotel. On another, she grabbed a pistol, aimed it at Desi's head and pulled the trigger. A tiny flame spurted from the muzzle, whereupon Desi casually stepped up and lit his cigar.

Those sympathetic to Arnaz claimed that he couldn't have survived without some kind of emotional outlet. After all, Ball was a strict taskmistress, one whose obstinance might have broken a less resourceful man. She was so thorough, so manic, so elated by her sudden power, that making the show perfect became an obsession. No one was going to stand in her way—and that included Desi, whom she constantly upstaged on the set and overruled off it, thereby leaving the impression (which persists to this day) that Arnaz was really a no-talent Cuban conga player who made good off his wife's talents.

After one too many confrontations, Arnaz, according to his memoirs, finally told his wife he'd had it. Lucy stared at him coldly and stormed off the set. At home that evening, she asked him if he'd meant what he said. When he nodded affirmatively, she sneered, "Why don't you just die, then?" Desi informed her he had no intention of dying. She cursed him and insulted him and threatened to leave him as poor as he'd been as a Cuban immigrant. She called him a two-timer, a drunk, and a bum. He had heard it all before; but instead of decamping to his bachelor digs as he usually did, Desi calmly produced a slip of paper bearing the name of a man with whom Lucy had been having an affair. It was obvious that there was no use trying to maintain the charade of marital bliss.

"I really hit the bottom of despair," Lucy said of the breakup later. "Neither Desi nor I have been the same since, physically or mentally, though we're very friendly."

Before their deaths, Lucy's and Desi's paths crossed many times, at family gatherings and for Lucy's various TV outings. Among those who observed them together on such occasions, it was often

remarked that they still seemed completely devoted. That makes it a little easier to watch them together as they frolic through sitcom eternity.

"Where did you dig up that bitch?" Bill Frawley often growled at his boss Desi Arnaz, when referring to his TV wife, Vivian Vance. (Frawley's other pet name for Vance was "Old Fat Ass.")

It wasn't just that Vance got on Frawley's nerves; he had despised the woman from the first moment he set eyes on her. And with some reason: out of her frumpy Ethel Mertz character, Vance was very much the grande dame. She'd come to TV from the Theatah, don't you know, and tended to think of herself as an artiste. But you'd be a little sensitive too if, like Vance, you suddenly found yourself catapulted into national prominence as the frumpy fictional wife of a humorless old poop. At sixty-four, Frawley was twenty-five years Vance's senior. "He should be playing my father," she often complained. Vance also deeply resented a clause in her contract that allowed her character to be written out of the show if anything happened to Frawley.

Nor was Frawley the only one to find Vance difficult. Although Lucy's eyes used to well up with tears when reminiscing about her after her death, she was often at odds with Vance during the show's run. "I'd tell you to go fuck yourself," Vance once screamed at the very pregnant Lucy after she berated her for missing a cue, "but Desi has obviously taken care of that."

Money was also a continual source of friction. Although Vance won many raises over the years, she was livid when she got wind of the sweet deal between Desilu and CBS that gave the Arnazes a multi-million-dollar profit even before the show went into syndication. She tried—and failed—to get a substantial salary increase at the time by threatening to have a nervous breakdown. The threat wasn't entirely idle; salary frustrations combined with her perennial second-banana status had cost Vance years of expensive analysis. Bart Andrews, the show's historian, says, "Throughout the series history, psychiatrists dealt with Vivian's dislike of Ethel by carefully disassociating 'the character' from 'the actress' in her subconscious."

Whatever Vance's ambitions, her fortunes were inextricably linked with both the real and the fictitious Lucy. Although she tried to do a star turn in her own sitcom (in the pilot episode of *Guestward Ho!*), she found herself "paralyzed out of Lucy's spotlight; when the show went on the air, it was with another actress (Joanne Dru) in the leading role." But at least she didn't have to put up with Frawley's perpetual rudeness. Toward the end of their onscreen tenure together, Vance and Frawley had stopped talking altogether. When asked about her later, he said, "I don't know where she is now and she doesn't know where I am and that's exactly the way I like it."

Thanks to his role as PFC Doberman on *The Phil Silvers Show* (commonly nicknamed "Bilko"), Maurice Gosfield, who had previously played only bit parts in the theater and radio, became a national celebrity. "Offstage, he thought of himself as Cary Grant playing a short, plump man," said Silvers, who evidently didn't think much of him. "He had no professional discipline. He fogged out on lines, cues, rehearsal time—with the most outrageous explanations. If he missed an entrance, he'd say he tripped over a sheet of paper." The only area Gosfield never disappointed in was slobbery. "His tie was always stained and his pants drooped. When he sat down to a meal he felt surrounded by enemies who would snatch his food if he didn't gobble it up first."

No matter. "Bilko" viewers couldn't get enough of Doberman, and so the writers kept making him the center of the action. After a while, he began to forget that his Dobermanisms were scripted (primarily by Nat Hiken). After an appearance on *The Ed Sullivan*

Show, Gosfield "began to have delusions," according to Silvers, "that he was a comedian."

Gosfield made guest appearances on several shows after "Bilko" but he was never called back. Soon, even those offers slacked off. "Most performers have gorgeous fantasies to keep themselves going," said Silvers. "Gosfield never accepted the realities of his appearance. And talent."

How's this for a Serious Actress's nightmare: shipwrecked on a desert island with six has-beens and never-weres? The stunning Tina Louise ended up stranded on *Gilligan's Island* after her promising film career was derailed. She wasn't happy and apparently made no secret of it, often remaining remote and cool to her fellow castaways. To her way of thinking, she had every right to be miffed; seeing as she'd signed aboard the S.S. *Minnow* under the impression that she was to be the show's star.

If Jean Hagen's name doesn't ring a bell, it's because her sojourn as Danny Thomas's wife on *Make Room for Daddy* was relatively short-lived. A serious character actress who'd been nominated for an Academy Award for *Singin' in the Rain,* Hagen resented playing second banana to a second banana—even though she received 7 percent of the show's profits and was nominated for Emmys in 1954 and 1955.

103

After three seasons, her character was killed off. Unfortunately, this led *Daddy*'s fans to believe that Hagen herself had died, too. Her actual death two decades later—after years of severe drinking and health problems—seemed redundant.

DOBIE: I'm Dobie Gillis. I think I love you.
THALIA: I'm getting nauseous.

That Thalia Menninger . . . she really knew how to hurt a guy. As the small screen's first Material Girl, the nubile Tuesday Weld evinced a meticulously authentic snottiness toward the libidinous Dobie Gillis. But it turns out that Tuesday wasn't acting; she found Dwayne Hickman to be every bit as icky as his small-screen alter ego. And the feeling was mutual. "She just wasn't a pro," Hickman said later. "Late to work, late getting back from lunch. No sense of responsibility to the show." And then there was that little matter of the ferocious dog Tuesday always made sure to bring to the set—a white German shepherd that snapped at the cast and bit the director.

But look, you can't blame Tuesday for putting on airs. After all, she had become an absolute sensation with the very first cold shoulder she gave Dobie. And the show notwithstanding, Tuesday was Hollywood's Girl of the Minute, the armpiece of choice for the town's grooviest bachelors—Lenny Bruce, Elvis, and even Ol' Blue Eyes—while Dobie (and Dwayne) were strictly kid stuff. Gossip columnist Louella Parsons clucked over her wantonness, calling her a "disgrace to Hollywood"; but Tuesday couldn't have cared less: like another *Dobie* alum, Warren Beatty, she was just biding her time on *Dobie* till she could land oodles and oodles of high-paying screen roles. And besides, by that point, she was already jaded, if only because she was dead tired, having toiled for years prior to *Dobie* as a child model. (She never forgave her mother for putting her to work so early.) Tuesday departed *Dobie* after its first season, only to go on to a string of disappointing films that didn't begin to measure up to her unique talents. She would return to the tube in later years in several made-for-TV movies, although she was noticeably truant in the recent Dobie Gillis reunion.

So you're this actor, see—an actor who's been around for a while, paid your dues. True, you're a little on the short side, not to mention a little short of hair. Okay, so you're not Brando—but you're not exactly Mr. Ed. But anyway, whatever you are, it's 1959, and after who knows how many years of mostly unheralded TV work, you've come up with the leading role in a modest little series called *Riverboat*. And who do they give you for backup? A guy several years your junior. A guy who really *is* Brando, or looks like him anyway—looks even better, as a matter of fact. The guy's name is Reynolds. First name, Burt.

So what do you do, if you're Darren McGavin and you've got to keep the spotlight off the hunk and on you? According to Burt, McGavin's stay-ahead strategy involved sabotaging him every time he was about to step in front of the camera: "We'd run through a scene a couple of times, and then just before the camera rolled, McGavin would say to me, 'You're not going to play it *that* way, are you?' What little confidence I had would go right down the drain. . . . He destroyed me."

To let off steam, Reynolds spent his leisure time knocking heads together in L.A. bars, eventually earning himself a reputation as a hothead and an ungrateful young man. Reynolds got so ornery that his part on *Riverboat* was minimized and his closeups eliminated altogether. Within a few months, he was written out of the series. Burt says that the bad rap he took on *Riverboat* kept Hollywood's doors closed to him for a long time afterward.

Of course, both men went on to bigger and better things: Burt to the centerfold of *Playgirl* and McGavin to practically every made-for-TV movie ever made for TV. Here's the best part: more than twenty years later, Burt's still miffed: "Let's just put it this way," he says. "McGavin's going to be very disappointed on the first Easter after his death."

The black family-based sitcoms of the seventies, *The Jeffersons* and *Good Times,* were TV milestones of a sort. Finally, blacks were to be allowed to be as goofy as their white sitcom counterparts, without having to conform to the oppressive stereotypes of *Beulah* or *Amos 'n' Andy.* The path toward more realistic treatment of blacks in continuing series had been smoothed in 1968 by the saccharine *Julia,* which for lack of a better description was classified as a sitcom. But *Julia* was so uplifting in its treatment of race that the only howls it provided were howls of disbelief and, on occasion, protest from the black community. (The NAACP, and at one point, Harry Belafonte, lobbied Diahann Carroll to abandon the role.)

No one could accuse CBS's *Good Times* of being uplifting. On the contrary, the character of J.J. (played to a pop-eyed, preening fare-thee-well by comedian Jimmie Walker), with his shady fast-buck schemes, prompted charges that the show was guilty of reviving the odious ethnic stereotypes of the bad old days. And therein lay much of the problem for its star, Esther Rolle, whose popularity on *Maude* had originally set *Good Times* spinning. "It's a matter of black pride," she said. "I resent the imagery that says to black kids that you can make it by standing on the corner saying 'Dyn-O-Mite.' J.J.'s eighteen and he doesn't work. He can't read or write. He doesn't think. The show didn't start out as that. Little by little, they've made J.J. more stupid and enlarged his role."

Perhaps more galling, however, was the fact that J.J./Walker had emerged as the show's undisputed star. That meant he got most of the yuks, most of the close-ups, and most of the scripted action. It also meant that Rolle and John Amos, initially the core of the show, were gradually eased into the background.

At the start of the 1975–76 season, John Amos aired his grudges and grievances with the show in a scathing interview in *Ebony* magazine. Not surprisingly, his candor didn't sit well with *Good Times'* creator, Norman Lear. He was promptly written out of the show as a runaway father. Rolle exited soon after, and suddenly J.J. became the head of the household.

Stung by the controversy, Walker lobbied to have his character smartened up a bit, and as a result J.J. was outfitted with a strong antidrug, stay-in-school rap. But nobody bought the new, improved J.J., and

105

Walker wasn't terribly effective at putting him across. But then, by this point, Walker was somewhat distracted, his head having been turned by competing ABC network czar Fred Silverman's promise of a lucrative deal for his own ABC series at whatever point the good times ended. Said one Lear associate, "Jimmie knew that no matter when the show concluded—that season or four seasons thereafter—he would have a pot of gold. ABC offered a lot of carrot money, and Jimmie had every incentive not to do a good job." *Good Times* dropped to twenty-fourth in the ratings during the 1975–76 run. The show continued to slide despite the return of Esther Rolle, who apparently managed to swallow her ethical objections. Ultimately, the only winners in the *Good Times* debacle were ABC and Silverman, whose wooing of Walker successfully disabled the powerful CBS time-slot challenge to their own top show, *Happy Days.*

You'd have thought if Gabe Kaplan was going to have a problem with any of his *Welcome Back, Kotter* co-stars, it would have been with Sweathog Numero Uno, John Travolta—seeing as how his popularity had eclipsed not only Kaplan's but the entire show's. That must have been hard on Kaplan, given that the series was based on his well-known comedy routine about growing up tough in the Brooklyn streets. But as it turns out, Kaplan's problem wasn't with Travolta but with Mrs. Kotter, Marcia Strassman.

In 1978, at the height of the show's huge popularity, Strassman was going around telling anybody who would listen, "I'm miserable. Gabe runs hot and

cold—one day he's your best friend, the next he's not speaking. Even blatant hostility would be easier to deal with. It's always been hard to act with him, especially in the intimate scenes. I hate the series. I pray every day for cancellation."

Eventually, *Kotter*'s cast and staff divided into two hostile camps—one pro-Kaplan, the other pro-Strassman. Ordinarily the star comes out on top of this kind of power struggle. And that's what most Hollywood insiders predicted with the *Kotter* fracas, particularly since Strassman rarely had more to do each week than say to her co-star, "So *then* what happened, honey?" But in addition to Strassman, Kaplan had managed to incur the wrath of the show's powerful executive producer, James Komack. (Not a good idea.) In truth, Komack had had problems with Kaplan right from the beginning. He was indifferent to Kaplan's brand of humor, and wasn't that wild about Kaplan himself.

With the cast in an uproar, Komack moved to undermine Kaplan by firing all of his writer/director pals—in other words, the people who made *Kotter* the "Welcome Back, Kaplan" show. Now that his backup was gone, Kaplan had less and less scripted business, and Strassman, after years of being practically invisible, suddenly became the focus of the show. With Kaplan disabled and Travolta off to greener pastures, the show was seriously wounded. It limped off the air after its fourth season, a stellar example of how off-screen feuding can kill off even the most solid hit.

You couldn't really blame *Tomorrow Show* host Tom Snyder for being miffed: He considered himself a Serious Journalist (even if he did spend most of his time fawning over celebrities or doing live remotes from nudist colonies). And yet here he was, former unchallenged solo ruler of the late-late-night no-man's land, sharing the airwaves with the prissy gossip columnist Rona Barrett, who'd been foisted on him by NBC.

Snyder made sure his audience got the message that he was thoroughly disgusted by Miss Rona's nightly kissy-kissy gossip installment. (Rona: "That's the news from Hollywood for tonight, Tom. See you tomorrow." Tom: "Not if I see you first, Rona.")

What with today's big-money stakes, broadcast journalists are usually too professional to let their animosities break through on the air. To watch *Good*

Morning America's six-year-long teammates Joan Lunden and David Hartman chattering away in their mock suburban living room, you would never for a moment have guessed that the two often sat in stony silence during commercial breaks. It turns out that Lunden resented the fact that Hartman monopolized all the hard-news stories, leaving her to cover the latest breakthroughs in oven mitts. Eventually Lunden, not nearly the delicate blossom she seems, demanded—and won—parity with Hartman in billing, though not in salary. Soon after, Hartman departed the show, his nice guy persona still intact, despite whispers from *GMA* staffers that he was, in fact, a power player reluctant to share even a sliver of the spotlight with a strong woman.

Poor Suzanne Somers. Okay, so she got a little carried away during her heyday on *Three's Company.* Thought she was Sarah Bernhardt or Lucille Ball or something. Okay, so maybe she wasn't a comedic genius, and maybe she did practically have to be fed every single line reading by the director or a cast member. But never you mind, because however she did it, Somers's Chrissy Snow was catnip to American audiences. The show was dreck, but viewers loved it—and her. A year after her series debut, Somers had replaced Farrah as the reigning TV sex symbol of the seventies complete with the full complement of posters, tee-shirts, and other trivial tokens of mass esteem. "If you've got it," she gloated, "bump it with a trumpet."

But Suzanne bumped it, it seems, at the expense of her co-stars, John Ritter and Joyce DeWitt—starting with a *60 Minutes* interview and a *Newsweek* cover portraying her as the show's top star. Fifty-five other covers that same year didn't help to calm Ritter and DeWitt down. Tensions escalated as Somers held up shooting to finish a feature film with Donald Sutherland. Somers then replaced her supermanager Jay Bernstein with her husband, Alan Hamel, who immediately demanded a piece of the action and a 500 percent raise (to $150,000 a show) for his new client.

By the fourth season, DeWitt talked to Somers only when absolutely necessary. But what really hurt Somers was that Ritter, with whom she'd been extremely chummy, was also now giving her the cold shoulder. "I can't say I've ever been friends with Joyce," she said later. "We've had an ego problem for five years. But John was one of my best friends." She tried to tell him that "I only wanted what I de-

served," but his only reaction was to "look at me and walk away."

As TV's quintessential dumb blonde, Somers came very close to superstardom. So how dumb was she? Not so dumb that she didn't know how to demand a great deal more money than her co-stars—but dumb enough to walk when she didn't get it. The truth is, Somers was an actress who'd kicked around a tad too long before Fred Silverman discovered her in a *Tonight Show* sketch playing (what else?) a bikini-clad bimbo. Her credits were modest, not to mention eclectic: a Mr. Clean commercial here, some skin modeling there. (Nude shots from leaner times showed up in the pages of *Playboy* and *High Society* at the height of *Company*'s popularity.) At her advanced age, she should have known better than to mess around with such a good thing. "She was too old when she came to me in the first place back in 1977," observed Jay Bernstein later. "You know, little lines around the eyes." And it was true in a way: as a woman in her thirties, with a teenage son, Somers might as well have been Dame May Whitty as far as

Hollywood was concerned—a town where a woman with "little lines around the eyes" is worth about as much as a secondhand Camaro. Of course, Farrah Fawcett, who is almost as ancient as Somers, had been able to bounce back from a similar series defection in 1977. But Farrah could discard her bimbo image by taking off her makeup and doing "serious" roles. Winning back Hollywood's respect has proved to be more difficult for Somers.

After three failed pilot attempts, she finally clicked in the syndicated piece of fluff called *She's the Sheriff.* But that show too bit the dust in 1989, after a couple of seasons. For now, Somers commutes the Vegas–Atlantic City circuit, where she sings "Feelings" to weekend junketeers—a fate Hollywood seemed to feel she deserved. Clearly someone as old as Somers should have known better: five years after her departure from the show, a *TV Guide* article entitled "The Rise and Fall of a TV Sex Symbol" was still gloating over her defeats, the hollowness of her life as a gambling-house chanteuse, and, most of all, those (gulp) little lines around the eyes.

Although George Peppard has long had a reputation in Hollywood for being cranky and cynical and something of a bully, he's managed to hold on to his name-brand status for years thanks to a kind of blond, bland boyish charm. But Peppard met his match when he met Mr. T.

Peppard signed on *The A-Team* as its big-name in residence and so-called Senior Member, but it wasn't long before he found himself being routinely upstaged by a pituitary case covered with more chrome than a '57 Chevy—the gouge-hall star, Mr. T. By the show's second season, T had scored a fat salary increase, his own line of products and First Lady Nancy Reagan sitting on his lap. As T's popularity grew, so grew his head; he took to putting on airs—like snubbing the rest of the cast and demanding all sorts of perks. This was simply more than Peppard could bear. Labeling T "an embarrassment," he complained bitterly to the show's producers, insisting that his part be beefed up along with his salary (which at a million a year wasn't exactly paltry to begin with).

The A-Team, so raucous in the beginning, was eventually felled by its stars' offscreen bickering. Peppard will no doubt bounce back with more schlock. But you have to wonder what will become of Mr. T. After all, the he-man business can be something of a dead end. (Just acting human would be a stretch for

T.) After a short run with an *A Team*–like series, *T. and T.,* Mr. T is back where he belongs—on the wrestling circuit and Saturday-morning cartoons.

Speaking of ambitious newcomers, how about Michael J. Fox? It took that little pisher only two years to convert what was originally intended to be a Meredith Baxter-Birney star vehicle into "The Michael J. Fox Show." Fox's emergent cult-idol status on *Family Ties* turned his TV mom into something of a fifth wheel. By *Ties'* fourth season, she had more lines in her hair-color commercials than she did on the show.

Amid growing rumors of friction among his cast, *Ties* creator Gary Goldberg denied that there was ever a conscious decision to magnify Fox's role to the detriment of Baxter-Birney's and Michael Gross's. But Fox's dominance was established right from the beginning: after the taping of the seventh episode ran twelve minutes overtime owing to the laughs generated by Fox (as Alex lost his virginity to a coed who shared his passion for economist Milton Friedman), Goldberg turned to Baxter-Birney and Gross and said gently, "If you want out, I'll understand."

It must've seemed like kismet—or something—when Pierce Brosnan was tapped to become the new James Bond. Brosnan had dreamed of playing Bond ever since he was a kid, and then too, his American series, *Remington Steele,* had just been cancelled by NBC. Add to that the pleasure of playing opposite a random sampling of female lovelies as opposed to his co-star of the previous three years, Stephanie Zimbalist. Not that he didn't like Zimbalist; it was just that they were, in his words, "diametrically opposed in everything from religion to philosophy to background." Aside from those trifling differences, they were best pals.

Rumors of discord between *Remington Steele*'s romantic leads had surfaced during the show's first season as the debonair Brosnan began attracting more and more attention away from the top-billed Zimbalist. There was also friction between Zimbalist and Brosnan's wife, who was known to be very ambitious in his behalf. In truth, Brosnan was pretty ambitious in his own behalf, figuring that if he was going to be a star, he might as well hire a press agent and start acting like one. Before long, he'd become the Hunk of the Year. "I have to do something," Zimbalist was heard to mutter, "or when this show goes off the air, all anybody is going to remember is that Pierce Brosnan starred in it."

Losing momentum rapidly after the marriage of the two leads during the third season, the show was stumbling toward its final episode when Bond quite inadvertently saved the day for Brosnan. Relieved, he returned to England, where he proceeded to wax unduly candid in interviews about both the show and his former co-star. But then, just three days before he was to sign on with Her Majesty's Secret Service, NBC decided to exercise its option to renew *Remington Steele* for another six episodes. Apparently, the prospect of Brosnan as Bond had suddenly revived the network's interest in both him and the show.

Ironically, the delay caused Brosnan to lose Bond to Timothy Dalton. And without Bond, Brosnan was no longer viable to the network as *Remington Steele.*

When Joan Rivers ankled *The Tonight Show* to launch her own copycat version for the Fox Broadcasting Network, she had all sorts of reasons to explain why, during what must have been weeks (if not months) of negotiations, she hadn't gotten around to informing her boss and mentor, Johnny Carson, of her plans:

1. Her advisors insisted she keep mum

2. She was afraid she'd blow her new deal

3. Johnny's hard to get through to

4. She meant to, she really did.

She acknowledged that it had been Carson who, out of the blue, had given her her first big break—"the moment when my life began, when seven years of rejection and humiliation paid off." But even so, she claimed, with the exception of their twenty-year on-the-air collaboration, she and Carson had never been *that* close. "Our personal relationship was curious. . . . Our friendship existed entirely on camera in front of America, and even then, during the commercial breaks, when the red light went off, we had nothing to say to each other." (The second Mrs. Johnny Carson—Joanna—remembers it differently: She says that Carson and Rivers had in fact socialized extensively over the years.)

So, why'd Joanie give Johnny the shaft?

Well, it seems that Joan had gotten the word (from either a secret memo or her hairdresser, depending on which account you prefer) that though her ratings had been sky high during the periods

109

she'd subbed for Carson, she was not among the candidates being considered to replace him upon his retirement from the show. Almost as galling was the fact that neither NBC nor Carson Productions had given her the kind of acknowledgment she craved: invitations to the yearly show party, antiques in her dressing room—that sort of thing.

But to really suss out what makes Joan Rivers tick, you have to understand what she suffered while clawing her way to the middle. For years as a struggling stand-up comic, she'd done her act (mostly "borrowed" material) at grind houses and scuzzy little clubs—only to be booed off the stage, bullied by sleazoid owners, and snubbed by other comics. By age thirty, show business considered her "too old, too shopworn, and too shocking. After years of being pampered, I'm still angry. . . . Whenever I ask for an extra bottle of champagne or a new bar of soap in my dressing room, what I really want is the respect that comes with it. I am punishing [the big guys] for the indignities I suffered getting started—for the nights I had to get dressed in filthy toilets, for all the disgusting dressing rooms where there was no toilet paper in the john."

There's every chance that Rivers was right, and she really wasn't in line to inherit Johnny's seat at *The Tonight Show.* In all probability, NBC understood what Fox did not: that Rivers's abrasiveness works best when juxtaposed with Carson's kind of cool. In any case, the tempest over a telephone call now blows the other way: it seems that Carson did not call Rivers when her husband, Edgar Rosenberg, committed suicide. "Who cares if he calls me?" she says. "It's *his* problem, not mine. His problem is how to put his head on the pillow at night. I met Edgar through Johnny Carson, and when Edgar committed suicide there should have been a note."

Temper tantrums. Screaming matches. Script stomping. Chair throwing. Bitching. Bickering. It was all just *too* delicious . . . those stories of the ego clashes between *Moonlighting*'s slick dick, Bruce Willis, and ice queen Cybill Shepherd. Although the show's executive producer, Glenn Gordon Caron, took the rap for *Moonlighting*'s frequent problems and costly production delays (at first, anyway), it was Cybill Shepherd who ultimately emerged as the villain-

ess in the piece. And that figured, really. After all, she'd always been the kind of girl we love to hate—that most dreaded of all creatures (particularly as far as Hollywood is concerned), the model-turned-actress, and, even worse, a wicked woman: the temptress who'd broken up the happy home of director (and noted shiksa-hound), Peter Bogdanovich.

By comparison, her co-star, the volatile Bruce Willis, came across as a pussycat, with everyone seeming to forget that he'd lost his cool a few times too—particularly during the show's second season.

Still, it was Willis who got all the juice—pulling down film offers, multimillion-dollar endorsement deals, and a recording contract. The *Moonlighting* set had been reasonably friendly until Bruce began to emerge as the hot property, leading Shepherd to suspect that all the attention he was getting was due as much to the hip-quipping way his character was written as to his own insouciance. She had become increasingly annoyed as she watched David become more adorable and Maddie more of a bitch. "Controlling the fantasy had a lot to do with it," Shepherd said of her battles of will over what Maddie should do or say. By this point, Cybill and Bruce argued about everything—including hair. "I purposely made a choice of an uptight, traditional hairstyle," she said a year after the show had gone off the air. "It made it funnier when you saw Maddie with her panty hose hanging down." But Bruce hated Maddie's straight-laced, matronly look and constantly criticized it, finally exploding, "You've got to do something about your hair!"—whereupon Cybill replied, "Well, at least I *have* some." And then, in the middle of the whole mess, Cybill became pregnant—causing many, including Caron, to fear that she intended to use her condition to get the upper hand on the show. For his part, Willis kept quiet during the ensuing chaos, although he was rumored to have Cybill's picture pasted on a dart board in his trailer.

With Cybill on the warpath, things got so bad that by December, producers were able to fill only one out of five air dates with a new episode. The following month's showing was only slightly better. Finally, at the beginning of the 1988 season, after Caron blamed $8 million worth of delays on Cybill, she hit ABC with an either-he-goes-or-I-go ultimatum. Figuring that Caron would look pretty silly in those slinky costumes, ABC opted to drop him and hold on to *Moonlighting*'s lissome blond star.

Now that *Moonlighting* is in total eclipse, Bruce Willis has managed to keep moving with strong box-office movies like *Die Hard I* and *II*. Cybill's return to the big screen in *Chances Are* was less well received, but then she may find it increasingly difficult to parlay her patented petulance into a long-lasting career. But no matter how well either she or Willis fares on the big screen, chances are that the on-screen chemistry will never be as right (or as wrong) for either of them again, and that *Moonlighting* will stand as their finest hour.

A veteran of both a hit series and a hit miniseries, the late Barbara Stanwyck was well acquainted with the slapdash nature of television by the time she agreed to do a star turn on *The Colbys,* the feeble *Dynasty* spin-off. Or so you'd have thought. (After all, *The Big Valley* wasn't exactly *Hamlet.*) However, appalled by the quality of the writing, "Missy" Stanwyck threw a *Colbys* script at producer Esther Shapiro's feet, calling it "garbage." In case Esther hadn't gotten the message, she went on to tell her that if Rock Hud-

Did The Colbys' scripts finish her off too? La **Stanwyck** with **Katharine Ross** on The Colbys.

son hadn't been dying when he did *Dynasty,* "the scripts would've killed him."

But it may be that the affront to Stanwyck's literary sensibility was less the problem than the blow to her vanity, which was severely wounded when the producers refused to give her a younger love interest. (Since hardly anyone was older than the eightysomething Stanwyck, that meant no love interest at all.) Nor did she find any gratification in the scenes she played with the ever-pompous Charlton Heston. "Chuck has a bad memory," she said of her co-star. "He still thinks he's parting the Red Sea."

111

TV GUIDE

15c

MLA

THE GREAT TV RUMORS

Have you heard the one about the kiddie kingpin who left orders that he be frozen after his death? The folks at Disney Enterprises certainly have—a few too many times, thank you. To this day, over two decades later, they regularly field calls asking about the rumor that their founder's body was cryonically preserved and buried in a secret location beneath Disneyland, until such time that a cure for cancer would allow him to be summoned back from that Great Theme Park in the Sky.

So how did the Waltsicle rumor start? As far as anyone at Disney can tell, it was cooked up by a few of the zany guys over in the animation department, who apparently thought it would be a goof to make light of their boss's death. (Their irreverence couldn't *possiby* have had anything to do with Uncle Walt's being a notoriously stingy authoritarian—perish the thought!) But despite the vigorous averrals of the Disney PR people lo these many years, the story simply refuses to defrost. How come?

Some rumors can kill a show, as happened when the manic kid-show host Pinky Lee blacked out in the middle of a live coast-to-coast telecast in 1955. Although Pinky's collapse was the result of a severe sinus condition and the pressure of doing six live shows a week, the next day it was widely reported that he'd suffered a heart attack—leaving millions of young fans and their parents to think the worst. Lee wasn't dead, but by the time he returned to TV after a year's hiatus, his career was.

For one thing, the putative link between cryonics and Disney was a logical one: why wouldn't Hollywood's Most High Wizard of Tech avail himself of what was at the time of his death (in 1966) California's highest technological weirdness? Besides which, to millions of children of all ages, Walt Disney *was* God. If anyone were capable of conquering the last great Frontierland, it makes sense that it would be the man who had reanimated Abraham Lincoln and put him to work as an amusement park attraction.

And then too, childhood idols are particularly prone to rumormongering. Any bogus tale, especially if alarmist in nature, tends to spread like wildfire across the little-kid network of classrooms, playgrounds, and backyard fences. Such stories, like the ones during the late fifties that had various Mouseketeers (usually Annette, Cubby and Karen, or mouske-leader Jimmy Dodd) killed in train or car wrecks, are apt to be quite difficult to extinguish once ignited. Another story, claiming that Jerry ("Beaver Cleaver") Mathers had been killed in action in Vietnam in 1969, was actually picked up and printed by a wire service. On the night it appeared, Shelley Winters, the noted actress/airhead, gave weight to the story by repeating it on *The Tonight Show.* Though

Mathers's parents denied the newspaper account in an official retraction the following day, they were nevertheless inundated with flowers and condolence letters for months afterward.

The response to the Jerry Mathers rumor reflected the nation's enduring affection for the character of the Beaver—by then, one of the very few cultural totems still capable of uniting a generation torn asunder by the war in Vietnam. Maybe it was some sort of collective longing for wholeness that made us believe that the jungles of 'Nam had claimed

> While tales of murder circulated through the Hollywood community following the death of George "Superman" Reeves from a gunshot wound to the head in 1959, the Los Angeles coroner's office ruled Reeves's death a suicide, the result of depression over the cancellation of his series. Apparently, though, Reeves had never been busier, having just agreed to a new project for his Superman Productions as well as a new film. By all accounts a lighthearted man with an impish sense of humor, Reeves was said to have been in particularly high spirits at the time of his death in anticipation of his impending wedding the following week.
>
> In calling Reeves's death a suicide, the Los Angeles police also chose to ignore damning information that one of Reeves's ex-girlfriends, Toni Mannix, the showgirl wife of Loews executive Eddie Mannix, had hounded him so relentlessly during the preceding months that Reeves had filed a complaint with the Los Angeles District Attorney's office; and that Reeves's will unaccountably left the bulk of his rather sizeable estate to that very same woman.
>
> Most of Superman's young fans remained unaware of stories linking Reeves with gangsters and gamblers and vengeful lovers. Instead, they believed rumors that had him falling to his death while trying to "fly" from a tenth-story window.
>
> "Let that be a lesson to you," their parents warned them. "Don't try that at home."

> The inspired bit of tomfoolery that had Rock Hudson "marrying" *Gomer Pyle* star Jim Nabors in a lavish double ring ceremony was contrived in 1971 by a group of gay pranksters in Manhattan Beach, California, who each year held a party around a different silly theme. One of the joke invites fell into the hands of a Los Angeles gossip columnist who wrote a blind item referring obliquely to the "marriage" of two Hollywood males, one "like the Rock of Gibraltar," the other "like your neighbor." The rumor gained momentum as all sorts of witnesses came forward to insist that they'd been present at the nuptials. (It didn't help that the rumor surfaced during a time when Hudson had become less discreet in his pursuit of casual sex.)
>
> Although Hudson's *McMillan and Wife* survived the uproar, Nabors's show was cancelled soon after. From that time on, Hudson didn't dare be seen in public with Nabors; he was reluctant even to go to Hawaii, where Nabors had a home. After issuing a statement denying the story, the two former friends did not speak for the rest of Hudson's life.

someone we could all join equally in mourning. Or maybe it was just that Mathers, having slipped into obscurity at about the same time that his childhood image had begun to flourish in rerun, had become the perfect target for a mass hallucination.

Once it was movie stars who spoke to the public's deepest longings, who fueled the fans' private and communal fantasies. But with fewer movies being made, TV stars in their ubiquity have eclipsed their big-screen analogues in the public consciousness. Yes, Mel Gibson may be every bit as glamorous as Gable, but he can't hold a candle to Roseanne Barr when it comes to titillating the masses.

Stars of TV's classic hits have now installed themselves in the pantheon of pop-culture deities. They're our gods, our mascots, our communal points of reference. And they are everywhere—on coffee mugs and tee-shirts, postcards and posters. There's no escaping them or the myths that surround them. Nor can the stars themselves do much to escape the rumormongering and myth-making that is proof of our obsession.

For the most part, however, the gossip that encircles TV stars tends to be less exotic and risqué than that surrounding their movie-star counterparts. We project film stars into dream scenarios as naughty as those they play in the movies. But that's not how we fantasize about TV stars; their off-screen characters are usually assumed to be as benign and circumscribed as their carefully scripted—and censored—roles. Such images can override even the most lurid tabloid tales. We're simply not comfortable envisioning those nice folks who come into our homes in any other way. Even now, as more and more revelations about the dark side of Johnny Carson surface, we resist them—not necessarily because we believe they're untrue but because we don't want to hear unpleasant things about a member of the family.

For all that they are less profane than their Hollywood counterparts, TV rumors are certainly no less apocryphal. Despite stringent libel laws and the stars' disingenuous protests and pleas for privacy, the Great TV Rumors continue to flourish just as they should—not simply because the public relishes them, but because a great many happen to be true.

If a rumor sounds too good to be true, that's probably because it is. It might contain a kernel of truth, but the rest is sheer invention.

It is true, for instance, that Loretta Young, the Bible-toting, Bible-quoting doyenne of TV, installed a "swear box" on the set of her show to fine anyone heard using profanity. But the story that a famed Broadway star once thrust a bill at her and said, "Here's ten bucks, Loretta. Now fuck off!" unfortunately is not.

Sitting too close to a TV screen can cause blindness.

The radiation emitted from a television's cathode rays can cause brain tumors.

An inebriated George (*Superman*) Reeves was killed while attempting to "fly" from a tenth-story window.

George Reeves inadvertently committed suicide while playing a game of Russian roulette.

George Reeves was murdered—either by an ex-girlfriend or by thugs hired by her jealous husband.

At the request of his mother, George Reeves's body was preserved for three years after his death in order to aid investigators seeking to track down his murderers.

Saturday-morning-kid-show star Pinky Lee died shortly after suffering a heart attack while delivering his theme song ("Hello, it's me/My name is Pinky Lee") during a live telecast.

Roy Rogers's horse, Trigger, and his dog, Bullet, are stuffed exhibits at the Roy Rogers Museum.

Walt Disney's body was cryogenically preserved and is buried in a secret location somewhere under Disneyland.

Desi Arnaz's fractured English was a put-on; the heavy Cuban accent he used for *I Love Lucy* was strictly a comic affectation that he was able to turn on or off at will.

I Love Lucy's Vivian Vance was contractually obligated to wear frowsy housedresses and remain twenty pounds overweight so as not to appear younger or more fetching than the show's star, Lucille Ball—who was a year her senior.

Lucille Ball and Vivian Vance were more than just friends.

Bitter and vindictive owing to his decline in popularity over the years, Red Skelton has vowed to take the tapes of his old *Comedy Hour* to the grave (much to the chagrin of the thirteen writers who worked on the show).

By his own admission, Milton Berle was—and still is—the biggest prick in television.

Columnist and *What's My Line* star panelist Dorothy Kilgallen died of a heart attack while reading in bed.

Dressed in a blue robe and (in the coroner's words) "extensive makeup including false eyelashes," Dorothy Kilgallen killed herself with an overdose of Seconal.

Dorothy Kilgallen's murder was staged to look like suicide by the CIA to prevent her from revealing the true story of the Kennedy assassination.

Gracie Allen was genuinely daffy.

Gracie Allen was a serious and often depressed woman (who also happened to have an ingenious sense of comedy timing).

Kid-show host Soupy Sales got the boot from New York's WNEW-TV after instructing his young viewers to reach into their fathers' wallets and send him all those "little green pieces of paper."

Dick Clark hates rock 'n' roll.

Lassie was a dozen different dogs.

Fury was a dozen different horses.

Flipper was a dozen different dolphins.

Depressed from lack of attention following the cancellation of his series, Flipper committed suicide.

The special effect that allowed Mr. Ed to "talk" was accomplished by the zapping of wires threaded inside his mouth with electric current.

When Mr. Ed "talked," he was in fact struggling to unstick peanut butter that had been plastered to the roof of his mouth by his handlers.

The theme song from *Mr. Ed* played backwards contains a satanic message that prompted all sorts of devilish mischief around the country during the show's initial prime-time run.

The real Mr. Ed did not die in 1978, as reported, but in 1973. The horse who continued to tour the country using his name was actually the horse who played Ed in the pilot episode.

116

Despite his whimsical sensibility, Walt Disney was a cryptofascist with radical right-wing views who made a policy of barring grown-up children with long hair from the Magic Kingdom during the sixties.

Jerry "Beaver" Mathers was killed in action in Vietnam.

Ken Osmond, the child actor who played the part of Eddie Haskell on *Leave It to Beaver*, grew up to be rock star Alice Cooper.

Ken Osmond grew up to be porn star John ("Johnny Wadd") Holmes.

Ken Osmond grew up to be an L.A. policeman.

Ken Osmond grew up to play the part of Eddie Haskell on *The New Leave It to Beaver.*

At the height of *The Mickey Mouse Club*'s popularity, several of the best-known Mouseketeers—including Mouseketeer chaperone Jimmy Dodd—were killed in a train wreck. Disney covered their absence by hanging new ears on a substitute squad.

It was the Mafia, not low ratings, that muscled *The Untouchables* off the air.

A black person once made an appearance on *The Lawrence Welk Show.*

Jerry Lewis's devotion to the muscular dystrophy cause is rooted in the guilt he bears from building his comic persona on spastic contortions.

Ken Berry and Bill Bixby are the same person.

Before taking up residence in his neighborhood, Mr. Rogers was a lounge singer.

Joan Rivers is a man.

Joan Rivers is a woman.

Herve Villechaize was pieced together from Phyllis Diller's old parts.

Ed McMahon's laugh is prerecorded.

During the last years of her life, Frances Bavier, Aunt Bee on *The Andy Griffith Show,* was a deluded recluse who believed she lived with Andy and Opie in Mayberry.

Don Knotts is Mick Jagger's father.

In real life *Captain Kangaroo's* Mr. Greenjeans was the father of rock-star brothers Johnny and Edgar Winter.

Many of the mind-boggling feats shown on *That's Incredible!* were staged much like magic tricks, if not completely faked by means of editing or special effects.

The chair-throwing incident between black leader Roy Innes and a white supremacist skinhead on the Geraldo Rivera show was a prearranged fight that got out of control and culminated in a broken nose for Geraldo.

Geraldo Rivera has been in contact with every major rock star who died of mysterious causes just moments before (or after) he or she expired.

Many of the "real life" participants on trash TV shows—self-proclaimed transvestites, child molesters, etc.—are actors.

Larry Hagman is interchangeable with the character he plays on *Dallas,* the mercurial J.R. Ewing.

Larry Hagman is a Malibu weirdo who spends his spare time hyperventilating on the beach and whistling instead of talking.

Morton Downey, Jr., co-wrote "Wipeout," the surf instrumental by the Surfaris.

Because of AIDS and Rock Hudson's death, Hollywood and the television industry had an unofficial blacklist of people who are known to be gay and people who just have question marks after their names.

Lou Grant was canceled not because of its declining ratings, as claimed by CBS, but because of series star Ed Asner's unpopular and highly publicized condemnation of America's military involvement in Central America.

There's a special camera lens that makes television actors appear twenty pounds slimmer. It's been used to flattering effect on *Designing Women*'s Delta Burke and *Moonlighting*'s Cybill Shepherd.

117

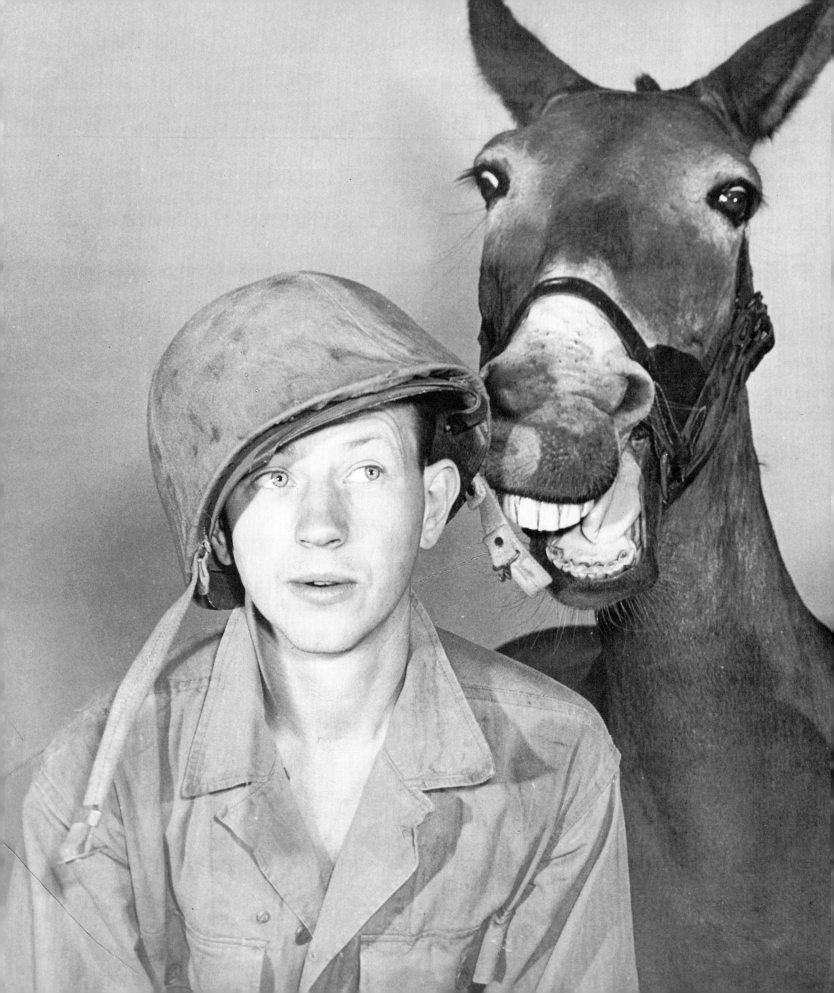

ALL IN THE FAMILY

A horse is a horse, of course, of course—unless it's not really a horse at all, but a . . . mule! That's right, a talking mule, as in *Francis the Talking Mule.* Yes, now it can be told: Television's *Mr. Ed* was nothing but a poseur, an also-ran who was given a species change by Hollywood imagemakers in order to enter the prime-time sweepstakes.

It wasn't hard to trace Ed's ancestry, since his TV mentor, Arthur Lubin, also happened to have directed all but one of the original Francis flicks. In most cases, however, the kinship between a TV show and its forebears isn't quite so obvious—lest its creators have to pay royalties to the prototype. The idea is to make just enough changes so as not to render a literal remake, but not so many that the product won't tap into a tested market. Or two. Such as with the "*Mary Poppins* meets *Bewitched*" premise of 1989's *Free Spirit* on ABC, whose lead character was both a British nanny and a whimsical witch. (And a model.)

This kind of gimmick-heavy plot line is what's known in televisionese as "high concept," baby—that is, one that's not only zappy but instantly recognizable as well (and preferably one that has clicked before). Ideally, that concept can be boiled down to a single buzz phrase, as in: "*The Lone Ranger* in outer space" or "*Magnum, P.I.* marries *The Flying Nun.*" (NBC's Brandon Tartikoff holds the title of King of the Come-ons for coaxing *The A Team* out of Stephen Cannell by requesting a show with "*The Road Warrior, The Magnificent Seven, The Dirty Dozen,* and *Mission: Impossible* all rolled into one with Mr. T driving the car" as well as for his classic description of *Miami Vice* as "MTV cops.")

As Fred Allen once said, "Imitation is the sincerest form of television." There's nothing new about borrowing (and stealing) concepts and plots and gimmicks; TV has always been a copycat medium. Right from the start it was a grab bag of ideas glommed from other show-biz genres: The comedy variety format of the Milton Berle and Ed Wynn shows, for example, was just burlesque minus the bimbos; sitcoms like *I Love Lucy* were transplanted radio comedies; and live TV drama was Broadway on a budget.

Of course, the richest and most deeply mined source of television programming is, was, and forever shall be the movies. The incestuous relationship between the film and TV industries began in earnest in 1955 when Warner Bros. moved into TV production with *Warner Brothers Presents,* a continuing dramatic series that alternated scaled-down variations on three of its old features (*Kings Row, Casablanca,* and a 1947 western called *Cheyenne*) on ABC. It was a beautiful system, really: all the studio had to do was dust off an old script and a few costumes and cast whichever contract players they happened to fit—in much the same way it had recycled back-lot odds and ends into low-budget B's during the forties. The same clichés that saturated second-feature westerns and crime melodramas turned up to haunt viewers on the small

119

screen; but this time around they were even hokier than the programmers that had played at the bottom of the bill at local Bijous. But quality wasn't a particular priority: The last thing studio head Jack Warner wanted was to forge an alliance with the demon box. The point was to lure audiences away from their TVs and back into movie theaters by touting the studio's newest theatrical releases with the glorified ten-minute commercial called "Behind the Scenes" that followed every show.

But then something completely unexpected happened: One of the three series (and the least likely at that), *Cheyenne,* became a runaway hit, a national sensation. Acting quickly, Warners did what it usually did when a particular formula clicked: It repackaged it into the next thing—in this case the westerns *Sugarfoot* and *Bronco.* Likewise, a second hit series for Warners, *77 Sunset Strip,* resurfaced as *Surfside 6, Hawaiian Eye,* and *Bourbon Street Beat*—all detective shows that were virtually interchangeable except for their locale (seen only on the opening credits), theme music, and cast of resident hunks. By using an assembly-line process—first to copy its own films, then to copy the copies if they happened to be successful— Warners set itself back on course toward its current position of industry dominance as well as establishing the hallowed tradition of television knockoffs, which, a few inspired innovations notwithstanding, has become the industry standard over the years.

This particular kind of imitation involves snatching a successful premise, from either a film or from another TV show, and rewiring it with a different set of characters. The show then pretends to be new and improved, although everything about it gives you a serious case of déjà vu (something like what you might have felt watching Laverne and Shirley wrestle with a speeded-up conveyor belt à la *Lucy*). Less insidious imitation obtains in the spin-off, which takes a popular character from a successful show, shuttles him to a new environment, and conjures up a new series around him (the way that *Laverne and Shirley, Mork and Mindy,* and *Joanie Loves Chachi* were all spun off *Happy Days*).

In fairness, it should be noted that the sudden appearance of a copycat series can be relatively innocent (or as innocent as a cutthroat competition between networks will allow)—a simple matter of an idea that has long languished in limbo finally getting the green light because something similar has broken through.

No matter what its permutations, when you're talking about imitation, homage must be paid to TV's copycat king, Freddie Silverman—the Man with the Golden Gut. Silverman polished the process of cloning hit programs while at CBS as a Saturday-morning programmer, later perfecting it when he decamped to ABC. It was Silverman who was responsible for spinning off *Laverne and Shirley* and *Mork and Mindy* from *Happy Days* (just as he had spun off *Rhoda* and *Phyllis* from *The Mary Tyler Moore Show* back at CBS); who molded *The Bionic Woman* from *The Six Million Dollar Man;* and who gave the world the singing, quipping, Bob Mackie–adorned TV duos of Sonny and Cher, Donny and Marie, and the Captain and Tennille.

Silverman spun and cloned and copied and recycled and rewrapped so many of his own hit shows that for a time it almost seemed as if all of ABC's shows and characters were related—members of some huge, loosely connected family. Once execs at NBC and CBS divined the power of the Silverman formula, they fell all over themselves trying to go him one better. Following Silverman's success with the three jiggling detectives of *Charlie's Angels,* for instance, NBC and CBS unveiled their own bouncing trios of stewardesses, beach girls, cheerleaders, and coeds. And it didn't stop there. So many Silverman formulas were appropriated that before long, he was virtually programming all three networks.

There are those (TV critics and other spoilsports) who deplore such video cross-pollination as a kind of pop-culture crime, a sinister practice that necessarily results in all TV programming being targeted to the lowest common denominator of public taste. Monday-morning programmers cry out for originality, but for this most populist of mediums, such lofty aspirations are absurd.

As the truest form of mass-market entertainment, TV can't really be expected to take risks. A small-screen presentation must tickle the network, placate the sponsors *and* Jerry Falwell, and somehow still manage to keep the folks at home awake. And then too, there are just so many harebrained housewives, nosy neighbors, genies, cops, and gumshoes to appease the insatiable programming lust of three networks, myriad international markets, and a bazillion cable stations.

So as you trace the genealogy of your favorites, don't be surprised at how many bear a striking (and rarely coincidental) resemblance to another show— or shows. The miracle is rather that any TV offering should ever be original or new.

120

James Garner in Maverick.

Errol Flynn in San Antonio.

121

Roy Huggins, who created *Maverick* for Warners, likes to remember the series as a unique invention—a western that sent up the genre with an offhand, self-mocking tone. The show's star, James Garner, recollects it differently. To his way of thinking, *Maverick* was not nearly so grand in its pretensions, but rather an outright ripoff of *San Antonio,* an old Warners western with Errol Flynn. He even swears that his dandified Maverick duds were the same ones Flynn had worn in the film. ''They used stock shots from the Flynn movie, so my clothes had to match up.'' According to sources at Warners, both men are right. In the typical Warner Brothers assembly-line manner, *Maverick* did indeed use stock shots from a number of its westerns, *San Antonio* included; but the story line and, more importantly, its droll tone were conceived by Huggins.

(Incidentally, a tussle between Garner and Huggins over the credit for *Maverick*'s success resulted in Huggins being put out to pasture.)

No Time for Sergeants

Gomer Pyle may not have rigged the barracks latrine seats to salute Sergeant Carter, but in every other possible aspect the relationship between the sergeant and his hayseed nemesis was strongly reminiscent of the hit comedy *No Time for Sergeants.* But that's no big surprise, since *Gomer* was a spin-off of *The Andy Griffith Show,* whose star was originally catapulted to stardom in the TV, then the stage, and finally the movie version of that very same play. In fact, *The Andy Griffith Show* was itself a *Sergeants*-style redo, with Andy reprising his role as the bumbling Will Stockdale turned sheriff down Mayberry, North Carolina, way. Over the years, Andy's deputy, Barney Fife, gradually began to outbungle Andy as Andy became less goony, thereby reconfiguring the basic formula yet again.

(An official spin-off series of *No Time for Sergeants* debuted on another network, ABC, the same month as *Gomer Pyle, U.S.M.C.,* but viewers were too smitten with the copy to bother with the real thing.)

122

The Andy Griffith Show

Gomer Pyle, U.S.M.C.

The Egg and I

Green Acres

Granny and Uncle Jed Clampett owed MGM's Ma and Pa Kettle a bucket of hog jowls for patenting the dim-witted Southerners they milked for nine ratings-busting years on CBS. Shucks, the Kettles had been exploiting hillbilly stereotypes since back before Jethro was in long—er, ankle-length—pants.

Petticoat Junction, Green Acres, and *Here Come the Brides* also made hay with Kettle-style rube humor.

And speaking of *Green Acres,* that show's city-girl-roughs-it-on-the-farm plot was lifted from a 1947 Paramount comedy called *The Egg and I* starring Fred MacMurray and Claudette Colbert, which also happened to mark the film appearances of Ma and Pa Kettle.

123

Is there anything more heartwarming than a houseful of young 'uns? How about a houseful of young 'uns who are—you guessed it—orphans!? And Mom and Dad just can't resist bringing home a new one every time they go out for a container of milk. Yes, there was always *Room for One More* on this saccharine series that had been adapted from the equally saccharine 1952 movie of the same name starring Cary Grant and Betsy Drake.

124

Timmy Rooney and **Andrew Duggan** in Room for One More.

The movie *Yours, Mine and Ours* borrowed heavily from a celebrated real-life marriage that united two huge families—with Lucille Ball as a widowed mother of eight and Henry Fonda as a widower with nine children. A year later the family and story line were scaled down to fit the small screen. That's the way they became *The Brady Bunch*.

It was the existential question of the era: Was *The Flintstones* an homage to or a rip-off of *The Honeymooners?* Whatever it was, producer-animators Hanna and Barbera never conceded the obvious similarities between the two. But the great Mel Blanc knew. The producers requested him to mimic Art Carney's Ed Norton voice for Fred Flinstone's neighbor, Barney Rubble. Unhappy with the idea of coopting someone else's creation, Blanc delivered his version with a slight change of intonation—but not so much that it wasn't obvious who Barney Rubble was meant to be.

Bell, Book and Candle

126

I Married a Witch

Like her luscious blond celluloid sisters Kim Novak (in *Bell, Book and Candle,* 1958) and Veronica Lake (in *I Married a Witch,* 1942), TV's earthbound witch Samantha Stevens brought an unwitting mortal under her spell in *Bewitched.* But by the time it reached television, the intriguing erotic possibilities of the big-screen premise had fizzled out, to be replaced instead by levitating telephones and other hokey video tricks.

Bewitched

Stalag 17

The sardonic sergeant, the Nazi dummkopf, and the wisecracking POWs of *Hogan's Heroes'* Stalag 13 were a few stalags too close to those of *Stalag 17* for the likes of Donald Bevan and Edmund Trzinski, the authors of the original Broadway hit (later a classic film starring William Holden). The judge in the plagiarism suit brought by the two men agreed.

Hogan's Heroes

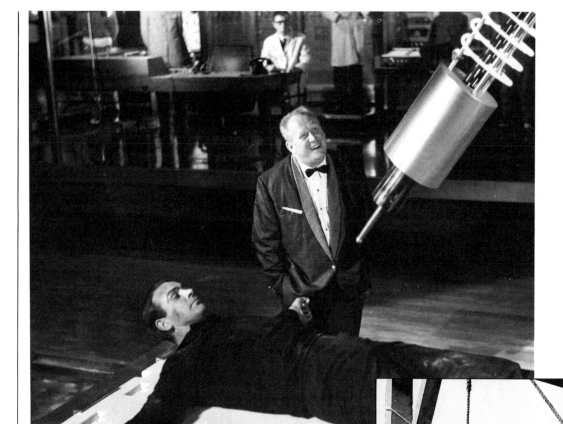

Goldfinger

128

The Man from U.N.C.L.E., The Avengers, and even The Wild Wild West all slyly exploited the secret-agent genre launched by the James Bond films. Just as Bond fought off the eccentric villains of SMERSH, superspies Napoleon Solo and Illya Kuryakin of U.N.C.L.E. did battle with the diabolical fiends of THRUSH—with the help of silly gadgets, exotic locations, and a bevy of Ann-Margret wanna-bes. With tongue planted even more firmly in cheek, The Wild Wild West utilized the same formula—a superspy battling supervillains with superweapons (vest-button bombs etc.)—only in this case, the action took place in the Old West as opposed to the Cold War West.

The Wild Wild West

Crocodile Dundee was still mucking about in the Outback back in 1970 when Deputy Marshal Sam McCloud first began meting out frontier justice to New York bad guys. Of course, McCloud wasn't exactly an original creation himself: The lawman from Taos, New Mexico, bore a striking resemblance to another rough-hewn lawman who, not coincidentally, had hit New York just two years earlier in a feature film called *Coogan's Bluff.* Like his predecessor, McCloud had originally arrived in New York to round up an escaped prisoner. After capturing his man, McCloud somehow found himself on temporary assignment in Manhattan's 27th precinct—where he proceeded to drive the New York City police crazy.

Dennis Weaver affected the same cowboy hat and sheepskin jackets worn by Clint Eastwood in *Coogan's Bluff,* but while he was no Clint Eastwood, he was believable enough to keep *McCloud* on the air for an amazing seven-year run.

McCloud

129

Coogan's Bluff

Ignoring early research indicating that test viewers thought he was too short and she was pimply and couldn't sing, Fred Silverman built a show around Sonny and Cher, custom-tailoring a music-and-comedy format that had Sonny as a dim-witted court jester and Cher as a tough-talking doll who cut her already diminutive husband down to size with carefully scripted ad-libs. And then he let *The Sonny and Cher Comedy Hour* grow for two years, until it blossomed into a top ten Nielsen show in 1973.

Three years later, Silverman recycled the *Comedy Hour* format for the toothsome brother-and-sister duo of Donny and Marie Osmond. A formula that aimed lightweight gags at the teenybopper contingent was adjusted to more closely resemble the Sonny and Cher setup during the show's second year, with Marie cracking wise and razzing Donny about his squeaky-clean image. (The revamping also included a sexy new look for the virginal Marie, courtesy of Cher's costumier, Bob Mackie.)

Later, with *The Captain and Tennille,* Fred Silverman was again trying to recapture the magic of that first *Sonny and Cher Comedy Hour.* Once again he set up comedic bits that were to be played off the couple's temperamental differences—in this case, the Captain's diffidence and Tennille's terminal perkiness. Silverman gave the show one of the biggest hypes ever, and, to no one's surprise, it bowed to a huge audience. But lack of tension in the interplay between the duo made the conceit fall flat, as, ultimately, did the ratings. Try as he might, Silverman just couldn't force-feed the formula to viewers yet another time. After all, they'd already bought the setup twice before—and from the same packager, at that.

130

Donny and Marie

The Captain and Tennille

Charlie Martin Smith, Paul LeMat, Cindy Williams, and **Ron Howard** in American Graffiti.

Before it became "The Fonzie Show," *Happy Days* was a period piece cum laugh track that recycled the early-sixties ennui of the 1973 film hit *American Graffiti.* The show also drew from a 1972 episode of *Love, American Style* that focused on the relationship between one Richie Cunningham and his friend Potsie Weber. Not coincidentally, both the film and the *Love* episode featured Ron Howard.

Each episode of *The Love Boat* intertwined three stories about voyagers on a cruise ship who suffered from various love-induced problems. After an hour's worth of lame jokes, pep talks, melodramatic sighs, and phony hugs, the afflicted passengers would miraculously come to their senses—but not before the requisite throng of bikini-clad bimbos had bounced by the camera.

ABC's Fred Silverman proclaimed *Love Boat*'s revolving vignettes "an innovation," but if you were paying attention, you knew that this format wasn't really new at all—it was *Love, American Style* on the high seas. While leading programming at ABC, Silverman cloned the "innovation" with *Fantasy Island* —and then cloned the clone with *Aloha Paradise.*

Like its two models, *Aloha Paradise* featured three revolving stories and an exotic locale populated by a star-studded cast consisting of unknowns and

old warhorses from the big screen (in other words, anyone who worked on the cheap). Although concocted by the same folks who created the originals, Silverman, Aaron Spelling, and Douglas Cramer, *Aloha* just couldn't sustain their lofty standards. In reviewing it, the *Los Angeles Times* called *The Love Boat* "a veritable *Citizen Kane* compared to this piece of nonsense."

In 1978 NBC ventured *Coast to Coast,* the pilot for an airborne version of *The Love Boat* that weighed in (and washed out) at a hefty $4 million budget. *Supertrain,* another variation on the same theme, made it to its own slot but stalled out as a hugely expensive fiasco. Who was behind *Supertrain?* You guessed it: Fred Silverman was at it again—this time cannibalizing his own spoor so blatantly for NBC that ABC might have had grounds for legal action if the show had been a hit. The shock waves from its spectacular failure resonated throughout Silverman's new network home, finally ending his reign as the knock-off king.

Henry Winkler, Marion Ross, Ron Howard, Randolph Roberts, and **Anson Williams** in Happy Days.

131

Charlie's Angels

Flying High

132

If *The Mary Tyler Moore Show* charted women's shaky progress in a man's world in the early seventies, it was ABC's *Charlie's Angels* that showed where women had landed in 1976. And where was that exactly? In a prime-time girlie show minimally disguised as a cop series. Week after week, the Angels could be found scantily clad, trapped on a cruise ship with a homicidal maniac; or scantily clad, busting a facelift farm run by the Mafia; or just about anywhere else—but always scantily clad.

The show's overwhelming popularity offered proof, according to its creator, Aaron Spelling, that "women could carry a TV show" (Sure they could, if they happened to be wearing bikinis.) *Charlie's Angels* also attested to the resiliency of the trio-of-cops formula that had been so successful for Spelling and Goldberg in *The Mod Squad,* as well as recycling the innovative concept of crime-busting female cops in hot pants pioneered by Angie Dickinson in *Police Woman* (not coincidentally one of ABC boss Fred Silverman's particular favorites).

In 1978, NBC and CBS scrambled to cash in on the formula as well. But all of the attempted imitations (*The Beach Girls, The Pom Pom Girls, The Roller Girls, The El Paso Pussycats,* and *Flying High,* to name a few) flopped. Still, the networks continued churning out pilots for the following fall featuring stewardesses, beach girls, cheerleaders, college coeds, and dozens of other variations on the female form at its nonthreatening best. Even the promotional themes of the networks dangled the promise of cheap thrills. "Turn us on, we'll turn you on," throbbed the CBS on-the-air jingle. But none were as good, or as bad—or, rather, as good-bad—as the original.

The sitcom formats that packaged second-string movie femmes into the lovable zanies of *My Little Margie, I Married Joan, My Friend Irma,* and *Our Miss Brooks* were fashioned after *I Love Lucy*—as were the later Doris Day and Debbie Reynolds shows. Debbie's show was even created by the same man who had overseen 153 *Lucy*s—Jess Oppenheimer. "They tried to put me in an old-fashioned Lucille Ball format," Debbie said later, "and I didn't like that one bit." (But that didn't stop her from doing it.)

By the time Laverne and Shirley got around to it, their Lucy-inspired shtick wasn't so much thievery as an homage, one that made no attempt to hide its inspiration. Why should it? After all, the show's executive producer, Garry Marshall, had recycled some of those same routines for Lucille Ball herself on *The Lucy Show.*

Visit to a Small Planet

Mork and Mindy, the Happy Days spin-off that featured comedy savant Robin Williams as a visitor from outer space, was to a great extent a reworking of My Favorite Martian—the premise of which had itself been reworked from Visit to a Small Planet, a Gore Vidal play that had been a minor movie hit in the fifties for another comedy alien, Jerry Lewis.

133

My Favorite Martian

Mork and Mindy

The action took place in the war-torn Pacific instead of postwar Kansas, but aside from that and Phil Silvers's dimples, everything else about *McHale's Navy,* which debuted in 1962, bore a striking resemblance to *The Phil Silvers Show* (1955–59). This time around it was Lieutenant Commander Quinton Mc-Hale (Ernest Borgnine) who was the fast-talking ring-leader with an endless supply of get-rich-quick schemes guaranteed to confound his long-suffering commanding officer and his lovable gang of enlisted loonies.

134

With its quick cuts and blackout sketches, *Hee Haw* came across as *Laugh-In*'s dim-witted country cousin.

The Phil Silvers Show

McHale's Navy

The castaways of <u>Paradise Lagoon</u> . . .

and of <u>Gilligan's Island.</u>

Just sit right back and we'll tell a tale . . . a tale of a British classic—a James Barrie play called *The Admiral Crichton* that made the voyage from stage to screen in the guise of several unacknowledged adaptations: *We're Not Dressing* (1934) and *Paradise Lagoon* (1957) and finally, to prime time as the immortal *Gilligan's Island.*

The premise which had wealthy travelers and their luxury cruise ship's crewmen all reduced to equal standing after being marooned on a desert island following a shipwreck had more resonance in England's caste-conscious society. But Americans enjoyed seeing the muckey-mucks get their comeuppance enough to make *Gilligan* a cult classic.

C'mon, folks, you know the tune: "Here we come, walkin' down the street/Get the funniest looks from everyone we meet/Hey hey we're the Monkees/And people think we Beatle around/And if you don't look too closely/*You* might think we're the Beatles too."

TV's Fab Four were obviously prefab and their show just an abbreviated rehash of *A Hard Day's Night,* but that was just fine with fans in that Beatle-crazy year of 1966.

In creating *The Monkees,* Colgems auditioned hundreds of young actors until they arrived at the proper mix of personality types to effectively mirror the real-life Fab Four. Mike Nesmith was the "smart" Monkee, the Lennonish leader; Peter Tork, the bashful Ringo type; Davy Jones and Mickey Dolenz a combination of Paul and George, with the British Jones initially slated to be the group's McCartneyish heartthrob. Witty directors like Paul Mazursky and Bob Rafelson were brought in to lend a little visual

The Monkees

The Beatles in A Hard Day's Night.

style to the random blackouts and musical bits that dominated the show.

Heavily hyped and carefully coordinated with the TV series, the Monkees' records sold in the millions. But the bubble burst when, during their first national tour, it was revealed that the boys didn't write or play any of their own material. If the fans felt duped, they weren't alone—the Monkees did, too. Going public with their dissatisfaction at a 1967 press conference, Mike Nesmith complained, "We're being passed off as something we aren't."

Demanding more creative control over their music, the Monkees attempted to shape themselves into a serviceable band. Their failure to do so led to friction with their Colgems mentors and ultimately to the group's (and the show's) demise.

Nesmith said later: "[The Monkees] were no more a rock band than Marcus Welby was a doctor."

Macon County Line

Smokey and the Bandit

The Dukes of Hazzard

137

Moonshine, car chases, and barefoot gals in cut-offs—the beefy hillbilly cousins of *The Dukes of Hazzard* (1979) had all sorts of things in common with the good ol' boys who had bumped around the country roads of *Macon County Line* (1974) and *Smokey and the Bandit* (1977) a few years earlier.

Dim-witted Sheriff Coltrane bore a strong resemblance to the redneck Smokey, just as the Dukes were spiritual sons of Macon's Max Baer, Jr.—Jethro on *The Beverly Hillbillies.* That made sense, since Jethro, or Baer, was the producer of *Macon County Line.*

The gangs at <u>Mary Hartman, Mary Hartman</u> (top) and <u>Soap</u>

138

A year before the off-the-wall gang at *WKRP in Cincinnati* fired the first salvo in the war to keep the airwaves free for rock 'n' raunch, a very similar group was engaged in the same battle on the big screen in the nifty comedy-cum-soundtrack, *FM.* When the premise moved to TV, *FM*'s cool Eric Swan (Martin Mull) had metamorphosed into *WKRP*'s even cooler Dr. Johnny Fever (Howard Hesseman), and Cleavon Little's Prince was reanimated as Tim Reid's smooth groover Venus Flytrap.

FM (top) and <u>WKRP in Cincinnati</u>

Despite Norman Lear's stellar TV track record, all three networks turned thumbs down on what would become his landmark sitcom *Mary Hartman, Mary Hartman.* But that didn't stop ABC from knocking it off after it became a runaway hit in syndication.

It billed itself as a breakthrough comedy, but *Soap* was 99 and 44/100ths percent pure *Mary Hartman, Mary Hartman*—in everything except the quality of its comedy. While *MHMH* used satire to send up soap operas and American social mores, the ABC show had all the subtlety of a blow to the head with a sledgehammer. Unlike the Norman Lear original, its attempts at ribald humor were often forced. And yet, as is so often the case, viewers preferred the bloodless copy to the real thing.

Animal House

In 1979 all three networks rushed to cash in on the success of the previous year's big screen comedy sensation, *Animal House. Brothers and Sisters* (NBC), *Coed Fever* (CBS), and *Delta House* (ABC) all had the ROTC geeks and the frat-house freaks and the prissy sorority girls. *Delta House* even had the same production team that had brought *Animal House* to the screen—as well as the rights to the movie's characters. What they didn't have was John Belushi. And that, as it turned out, was everything.

Delta House

139

Brothers and Sisters

Stranger Than Paradise

140

It was perfectly stranger than paradise. What better source material for TV to plunder than a critically praised, but little-seen, low-budget movie? The 1986 sitcom *Perfect Strangers* combined the character dynamic of Jim Jarmusch's 1984 sleeper *Stranger Than Paradise* with a generous helping of *Saturday Night Live*'s Wild and Crazy Guys by way of Bronson Pinchot and the hilarious mystery accent ("to what are you pertaining?") he'd invented for a small but memorable part in *Beverly Hills Cop.*

Danny Ackroyd and **Steve Martin,** Saturday Night Live's Wild and Crazy Guys

Bronson Pinchot and **Mark Linn-Baker** in Perfect Strangers

Cos and Company

141

Critics often accused *The Bill Cosby Show* of being *Father Knows Best* in blackface. But *Charlie and Company,* the *Cosby* knockoff with Flip Wilson, was more like *Father* than *Cosby* ever was. If anything, *The Cosby Show* was a spin-off of Cosby's Jell-O ads.

Flip and Family

YOU CAN'T DO THAT ON TV

Original Sin, Mistress, Naked Lie, The Sex Tapes, Death of a Centerfold . . . coming attractions at the Pink Pussycat Theater? Not exactly. File these come-ons under the heading of another kind of cheap thrill: the made-for-TV movie. But don't get the wrong idea. Though they may sound like run-of-the-mill sleaze, they are in fact hard-hitting "reality-based" exposés that point up all sorts of social ills.

True, The Sex Tapes featured a scene with a leather-clad vixen using a riding crop to discipline a paunchy man wearing only boxer shorts and a dog collar. But before you jump to any conclusions, you should know that the dominatrix was really an assistant D.A. gone undercover to get to the bottom of a series of blackmailings and murders. Now that's the kind of socially redeeming message you won't get at the Pink Pussycat. TV and X-rated movies may share similar interests, but TV distinguishes itself from unadulterated smut by taking a moral stand on the distasteful goings-on it portrays.

The networks' desire to titillate while at the same time toeing some sort of subtle moral line has given rise to a unique kind of video pandering whose unstated rule is that murder, mayhem, and graphic violence are acceptable . . . so long as they're "suitably" portrayed. Case in point: A 1989 CBS ruling allowed the Vietnam drama Tour of Duty to show bodies being blown up—but not falling to the ground. A delicate distinction to be sure, but perhaps we should be grateful for any display of restraint. As for sex, the prevailing sensibility is more or less that of an old Doris Day movie. It allows for lots of leering, double entendres, and in recent years, the occasional heavy breathing interlude that melts into the typical Hollywood-style fuzzy fade-out, but never (ever) nudity or simulation of the Real Thing.

The roots of this particular kind of video hypocrisy go deep: Lucy Ricardo wasn't permitted to be "pregnant" on I Love Lucy, for example—instead she was pronounced "expectant" (or "spectin' " according to Ricky). And such prudishness has proved long-lived, too: Almost fifteen years later, Mary Richards was allowed to be a single woman striking out on her own after a failed romance, but she still couldn't be a divorced woman in that same situation. By the late 1970s, starlets were allowed to "jiggle" their unfettered body parts at the camera, though they were still not allowed to flash their privates.

There was a time when the networks felt they had a mandate to teach and enlighten, as well as to entertain—or so they occasionally felt called upon to claim. But that was before the ratings survey called Sweeps Week and the proliferation of cable. The uncut theatrical movies aired on premium cable channels have catapulted nudity, semiexplicit sex, obscenity, and remarkable amounts of authentic-looking gore into the nation's living rooms. This brave new world has sent the networks scrambling in a frantic attempt to hold on to their audiences and, more specifically, to the revenues from their sponsors' advertising dollars.

Naturally, the networks couldn't compete with cable when it came to sexual explicitness and exposed flesh, but if they couldn't show it, they could talk about it. And talk they did. The upwardly anguished baby boomers of thirtysomething debated the merits of sex while using a diaphragm; the sophisticates of Tattinger's engaged in droll banter about impotence; and the cowboys in Lonesome Dove were constantly moseying off with the town whore for a "poke."

But those exchanges seemed tame compared to the anarchy that prevailed in the late eighties, after the Standards and Practices departments at the three majors were subverted by the drastic financial cutbacks that accompanied corporate takeovers and overhauls. With the blue-pencilers rendered virtually powerless, all heck broke loose. Saturday Night Live revelled in the humbling of its longtime nemesis by doing a sketch in which four apparently naked men used the word penis some thirty times in a period of three minutes.

And then there was Married . . . With Children with its jokes about bowel movements and vibrators. One particularly notorious episode dealt with a camping trip during which three women all started their menstrual periods simultaneously. Another featured this exchange between Al and Peg Bundy and their neighbor:

MARCY: . . . You know what would happen if men had breasts?

AL: We wouldn't need women anymore?

PEGGY: And if you had what other men have, I wouldn't need batteries.

AL: So *that's* what happened to my Die-Hard.

For one Michigan matron, this particular bit of business was the last straw. The subsequent protest and threatened sponsor boycott mounted by Terry Rakolta, a wealthy mother of four with big league Republican and conservative connections, very nearly killed off the show, and in the process shook the television industry to the core by demonstrating the power of a vocal, and vociferous, minority.

Faced with conservative outcries against "trash television," ABC dropped two bought-and-paid-for shows after nervous advertisers shied away from them. The Spelling-Goldberg company withdrew the medical drama *Nightingales* after nurses' unions decried the show's depiction of Women in White as *The Golddiggers Meet Dr. Kildare.* And Norman Lear killed a new sitcom, *Mr. Duggan,* after black elected officials complained about its unflattering portrait of a black Congressman. By contrast, the Fox channel hung tough during Rakolta's *Married . . . with Children* protest, refusing to take it off the air, even after the withdrawal of sponsorship by Warner-Lambert, the pharmaceutical giant. (But then, *Married* was the fledgling network's highest rated prime-time show. And by that point the controversy had propelled it from cult status to a full blown hit, so they really had no choice.)

Practically speaking, given the queasiness of advertisers and the continual (if lessened) vigilance of in-house censors and government regulators, the networks found themselves in a quandary: They couldn't go far enough to satisfy those with an appetite for true raunch, yet they had already gone too far to suit the media watchdogs of the New Right.

Although networks and studios denied giving in to pressure from conservatives and special interest groups, protests did sometimes succeed in changing the content of what got on the air. An episode of *Midnight Caller* that centered on a bisexual AIDS-infected man who continues to have sexual relations with a large number of men and women provoked a flurry of protests by ACT-UP (the AIDS Coalition to

Unleash Power). Fearful that the show's sensationalist treatment of the issue would lead to a greater risk of discrimination and violence towards those with AIDS, ACT-UP activists disrupted the filming of the scene showing the murder of the AIDS carrier and provoked the Mayor's office in San Francisco (where the show is shot) to step in and try to mediate the dispute. The script was changed significantly as a result—although not enough to satisfy the activists.

In truth, it wasn't just special interest groups and New Righters who were turned off by what they saw on TV; there was something to make everyone—even First Amendment groupies—cringe, particularly on cable. The talk shows broadcast by Public Access channels, particularly those in New York and L.A. hosted by Ku Klux Klan imperial wizards and pornographic strippers, not to mention the graphic commercials for phone sex ("Call 519-PISS"), made even staunch libertarians secretly long for the days of Lucy and Ricky's twin beds.

Despite the (almost) anything-goes sensibility that saw television standards take a serious turn south in the late eighties, don't look for the networks to get into true, hard-core raunch in the upcoming decade for a variety of reasons. Old habits die hard, and the Big 3 are loathe to abandon their self-proclaimed image as guardians of the public morality. The cable channels have their niche, and network television has its own—much bigger, and much more heavily supported by big bucks advertising. Advertisers still expect network television programming to conform to the rules of taste and decorum that befit its status as a "guest in people's homes."

And then, too, the controlling powers understand —if only tacitly—that television is a "passive" medium; its ultimate role that of a baby-sitter for the brain. It functions as a relaxing "pastime" for those occasions when people have nothing better to do. The last thing most viewers want is to be jolted out of their Barcaloungers by what they see on the tube.

For the time being, networks continue to walk the line between the high-minded and the scuzzy, creating all sorts of interesting interludes along the way. Here, then, is a brief catalogue of some of the more bizarre embarrassments and miscues, along with several martyrs to the cause and a few downright cryin' shames that have been born of television's fractured sense of righteousness.

144

Because of their host's concern for propriety, the women who appeared on *The Ed Sullivan Show* were required to present their costumes for advance inspection by him or his producer. A prude (as well as a prune), Sullivan saw to it that his wardrobe department kept artificial flowers and yards of netting in every shade and color to stuff into those necklines he considered too revealing. These makeshift alterations sometimes ruined costumes that had cost thousands of dollars. "This is television, not burlesque!" he would bark whenever the stars balked. Most capitulated—with the exception of Jayne Mansfield, who managed to divert attention away from her drop-dead dress by showing it to the producer while naked. Singer Dorothy Sarnoff didn't get off so easy: She ended up having to wear her elegant gown backwards.

Like Ed Sullivan, Lawrence Welk acted as his own arbiter of taste in regard to the costumes worn by the members of his TV "family"—insisting particularly on a high degree of modesty for his female performers. Welk's demand that the Lennon Sisters wear frilly little-girl dresses well into their teenage years contributed to their eventual departure from the show. Diane Lennon, who was still wearing crinolines and puffed sleeves at the age of nineteen, recalls the disagreements over clothes as the most unpleasant aspect of their years with Welk. "He'd practically raised us," she says, "and he just didn't want us to grow up." Welk also lost his popular "Champagne Lady" Alice Lon over a tiff about the length of her bouncy circular skirts.

Manufacturers and advertising agencies also got to put in their two cents' worth about television fashions. It was a sponsor, for instance, who saved the nation from potential moral turpitude when he cautioned Carl Reiner to watch the "undercupping" on Laura (Mary Tyler Moore) Petrie's "behind."

As the Standards and Practices departments of the networks became more powerful, censors too spent a good deal of time scrutinizing the subtleties of women's dress. . . .

There wasn't even a hint of sex among the castaways who spent three long years stranded on Gilligan's Island, but CBS censors nevertheless objected to Tina Louise's low-cut dresses and Dawn Wells's exposed navel. For some reason, the navel became a virtual Maginot Line for network censors during the late sixties and early seventies—it simply wasn't to be crossed.

Cher had continual battles with CBS during the run of *The Sonny and Cher Comedy Hour* over her Bob Mackie gowns with their bare midriffs. In trying to get around their restrictions, she ended up uncovering practically every other part of her body. Eventually her navel got equal time after it was determined that Cher's exposed flesh was the *Comedy Hour's* major attraction.

Once one navel surfaced, others did as well, leaving this nagging question: Did genies not have navels? Barbara Eden obscured her navel with draped chiffon on the show, and retouchers eliminated it in photographs.

Sammy Davis, Jr., in a scene from ''Auf Wiedersehen'' on The General Electric Theatre.

146

Those so-called Golden Days of Television weren't so golden for everyone—particularly anyone who happened to be black. As late as 1957, Sammy Davis, Jr., the hottest star on the nightclub circuit, had to lobby the William Morris Agency long and hard to get him booked on a dramatic series. Darned if they didn't land him a part—and on the prestigious *General Electric Theatre* at that. And darned if Sammy didn't turn in a heart-tugging performance that astonished industry insiders. All he had to do from that point, it seemed, was sit back and prepare to field his next offers. But, unfortunately, Sammy had violated a social taboo, and once again talent was made irrelevant by race. It turned out that Sammy's friendship thing with Columbia's top female star, the luscious and extremely white Kim Novak, made Kim's boss, the notoriously venal Harry Cohn, mighty mad—so much so that he suffered an apparent heart attack upon getting the news.

In his column, Walter Winchell let it be known that Cohn had requested that certain Chicago associates, most notably mob kingpin Sam Giancana, persuade Sammy to get over Kim real quick—which they supposedly did by giving Davis, who had only one

eye, the option of going for none. Coincidence or not, Sammy got the urge to marry a black dancer from his nightclub revue a few months later. But his sudden change of heart didn't occur soon enough to save his *General Electric Theatre* episode from being shelved without explanation.

In addition to the problem with Kim, there was also pressure brought to bear by GE, which was concerned about the impact of Davis's appearance in the South, where it sold 63 percent of its product. Threatening to take the whole affair public, William Morris coerced Universal, which produced the show for GE, into reinstating the Sammy episode into the following season's schedule. It did—and the response was ecstatic. Even so, it would be many more years before a black actor (Cicely Tyson) became a regular on a dramatic series (*East Side, West Side*), and another year after that before a black actor (Bill Cosby) received equal billing on a TV series (*I Spy*).

Bowing to pressure from the NAACP and other groups, CBS yanked the popular all-black sitcom *Amos 'n' Andy* from its network lineup in 1953 after only two seasons because of its allegedly degrading and demeaning depiction of blacks. The show's sponsor, Blatz Beer, also yielded to protests and withdrew its sponsorship. The reruns found a huge new audience in syndication where the show remained until 1966 when, at the height of the civil rights movement, CBS removed all copies of the show from both domestic and overseas markets and, in fact, made it unavailable for any broadcast purpose whatsoever. Today pirated versions of *Amos 'n' Andy*'s thirty-four episodes remain a dirty (and hilarious) little secret reserved for savvy videophiles.

Ed Sullivan got plenty of hate mail, especially from his southern viewers, for his affectionate embraces of black performers like Pearl Bailey following their numbers. Despite those protests, and others, blacks showed up with some regularity on variety shows in the fifties. But that didn't mean that white America was ready to invite one of them into their living rooms on a weekly basis—not even an ''acceptable Negro'' like the brilliant singer-pianist Nat King Cole who, in 1956, became the first African American to host his own thirty-minute TV show. One of the few black entertainers (along with Louis Armstrong and Ella Fitzgerald) to make the transition into

Nat King Cole on The Nat King Cole Show

white nightclubs and radio, Cole had a graceful, easy-going, urbane manner that made him a natural in front of the cameras. As the self-proclaimed "Jackie Robinson of television," he put on inspired shows that brought together big-name musicmakers for historic jam sessions. (The surviving kinescopes of the show preserve mind-blowing rave-ups featuring the likes of Ornette Coleman, Stan Getz, Coleman Hawkins, and Nat on piano.) But critical acclaim and a reasonably broad-based following were not enough to sell to advertisers who feared he could never survive in the southern television market. And, in fact, some NBC affiliates in both the South and the North refused to carry the show. Hugely disappointed and frustrated, Cole gave up the show after its first year. It was almost a decade before a black performer would again host his own variety show (the short-lived *Sammy Davis Jr. Show*), and yet another four years before the black comedian Flip Wilson would carve out a solid weekly niche on the airwaves in 1970.

In 1968, a scene from Petula Clark's TV special *Petula* had to be reshot because Clark had had the temerity to hold guest star Harry Belafonte's arm during a musical number—thereby sending the sponsor, the advertising agency, and the network into a tailspin. It was feared that mere touch might suggest the idea of a sexual attraction between the two that would shock and alienate the vast TV audience.

Robert Culp was the intended star of the action-drama *I Spy*. (After all, the show was called *I Spy*, not *We Spy*, and in the opening credits, only one silhouette—Culp's—was shown playing tennis, then trading a racket for gun.) But it was obvious right from the start that without the cool, funny support provided by his partner Bill Cosby, the *I Spy* hour would be a very long one.

He may not have had top billing but Coz got all the attention and all the awards. In fact he so dominated the show that Culp seemed to become him, mimicking his gestures and style of speech—which he still does today. But black groups criticized the fact that Scotty wasn't more militant. And how come he never got the girl?

At first a love interest for Alexander Scott was ruled out in order to combat, in Cosby's words, the image of the "sex-crazed Negro." But eventually, Coz, who had deliberately wanted his character to be "sterile," began to request some romance in the scripts—but not with a white woman. "As long as I'm on the screen, I will never hold or kiss a white woman. Hey, our black women have nothing to look forward to with films, nothing to identify with. . . . So as it is, I want to be seen only with our women, black ones." And so, when the time was deemed right, Scott did get a share of the ladies. And for the first time on a weekly series, young black actresses had more to do than play the part of maids or secretaries.

With *I Spy* a hit, more opportunities in television were made available to black writers, technicians, and actors. At *The Dick Van Dyke Show*, Sheldon Leonard hired Godfrey Cambridge to play Harry Bond, secret agent, in an episode called "The Man from My Uncle." And following the Cosby lead, Greg Morris was tapped to co-star on *Mission: Impossible* as the brainy electronics wizard.

The Culp and Cosby duo also paved the way for shows that experimented with white and black themes. Only after the inroads created by *I Spy* could there have been a television offering like *The Outcasts* where Otis Young played a former slave and Don Murray a bigoted cowboy.

147

Patty Duke and **Al Freeman, Jr.**, in My Sweet Charlie.

148

The critically lauded TV movie *My Sweet Charlie* (1970) featured Patty Duke as a white southern unwed mother who falls in love with a black attorney, played by Al Freeman, Jr. Four years later, another TV movie entitled *Wedding Band* paired the revered black actress Ruby Dee and J. D. Cannon as an older couple involved in an interracial romance in South Carolina in the early 1900s. Several ABC affiliates preempted (read censored) the show.

It was 1977 before a TV show actually attempted to suggest romantic passion between races. The TV movie, *A Killing Affair,* starred Elizabeth Montgomery and O. J. Simpson as police officers who fall in love during their tours of duty.

In 1986, Philip Michael Thomas and Lesley Ann Warren co-starred in *A Fight for Jenny,* a true story about a southern couple sued for child custody by the woman's ex-husband because she has become involved in an interracial marriage. Unlike previous efforts, *Jenny* made an attempt to show lusty, true-to-life love scenes.

Interracial relationships have made an appearance on such prime time shows as *WKRP in Cincinnati, Knots Landing, Dynasty,* and *The Jeffersons,* where the pairing of the white Tom and black Helen Willis was often the butt of bigoted George Jefferson's jokes. Rarely, however, were these liaisons allowed to sizzle with the intensity of noninterracial relationships. For example, you never saw these couples engaged in lovemaking. Instead, they just talked a lot—as on the 1985 season of *Dynasty,* where Diahann Carroll and Ken Howard spoke endlessly about their tempestuous past.

At the end of its second season in 1988, *L.A. Law* mounted an interracial romance between the brash black attorney Jonathan Rollins and the young white lawyer Abby Perkins that didn't shy away from torrid love scenes. The couple was forced to fight prejudice within their firm, as well as from Abby's young son. The gutsy plot line was just what fans had come to expect from the ground-breaking show, and yet the *L.A. Law* bosses were willing to venture it only with a secondary character like Abby as opposed to one of the show's top stars, like Susan Dey, for fear of losing her to negative viewer response.

You expect the networks to shy away from interracial romance on prime time, but love isn't even allowed to be color-blind on the soaps, where, ordinarily, anything goes. Not that they haven't tried . . .

In 1968 ABC broke ground on daytime TV by incorporating an "Imitation of Life"-inspired story line that had a character named Carla Benari (Ellen Holly) fall in love with her boss, a white doctor. That was fine with viewers until they, along with the doc, discovered Carla was really Clara Gray, a black woman. One outraged ABC affiliate canceled the show in protest.

In 1977, NBC once again dared an interracial plot on *Days of Our Lives.* She was black, he was white, and they got around to kissing maybe four times a year. The story was abruptly halted when marriage was discussed and fans wrote protest letters to the show.

Things are bound to have improved since then, you say? No such luck. As recently as 1989, interracial romances on both *All My Children* and *Ryan's Hope* were aborted just short of the bedroom. The networks attributed the sudden romantic reversals to lack of ideas and chemistry, but one actor said it was because of—surprise!—negative viewer response.

(By the way, not all the opposition to interracial plots came from whites. It seems that black women were often upset by—and resentful of—these story lines because they usually paired black men and white women.)

Allan Burns and James Brooks of *The Mary Tyler Moore Show* first conceived Mary Richards as a thirty-year-old divorced woman living in Minneapolis. By making her an assistant producer at a fictitious TV station her role directly challenged the three prevailing female stereotypes in prime time: the zany incompetent personified by Lucy, the Donna Reed–style happy homemaker, and the brain-damaged Golddiggers of *The Dean Martin Show.* While Marlo Thomas had broken ground on *That Girl* in 1966 by showing that a single woman could exist on TV, the character she played was still decidedly a girl, and her career often seemed little more than a cute hobby meant to occupy her time until she settled down with her "fiancé," Donald. Mary, on the other hand, would be appropriately ambitious about her career, in some

149

cases putting it before anything else. To the CBS programming hierarchy this was heresy. Brooks and Burns were told, "There are four things Americans can't stand: Jews, men with mustaches, New Yorkers, and divorced women." As a compromise, they ended up transforming Mary into a woman who was striking out on her own after having just ended an affair. This prospect amused MTM boss Grant Tinker, since to his mind the new Mary sounded more promiscuous than the original.

Oscar Levant during a moment of relative calm on The Oscar Levant Show.

150

Oscar Levant liked to say that he was perfectly happy as long as he was unconscious. And in order to stay that way, the noted pianist/bad boy medicated himself for depression and paralyzing stage fright with a staggering quantity and variety of prescription drugs, finagled from a battery of Beverly Hills doctors. In 1956 Levant, who had virtually withdrawn from public life, after being bounced from the concert circuit by the musicians' union for unprofessional behavior, overdosed on a drug called paraldehyde in what the papers later characterized as a suicide attempt—but was more likely a case of Levant trying to stay happy.

After his recovery, television station KCOP in Los Angeles, inspired by Levant's legendary appearances as a guest on the prime-time *Jack Paar Show,* lured him back into the spotlight by giving him his own weekly show—which was to be performed live, in front of an audience. It was the perfect setup for Levant: He could play a little piano and free-associate his way through any subject that caught his fancy, spouting intellectual cant one second and insulting whatever celebrity or politician (particularly Republicans and then-President Eisenhower) came to mind the next. Surrounding himself with his favorite kind of people—women—he played host to a sparkling array of Hollywood stars as well as some of the most famous intellects of the day: Linus Pauling, Romain Gary, Aldous Huxley, and Christopher Isherwood among them.

The show was a sensation, and Levant pronounced himself "reborn." In order to still the weekly pangs of video birth, however, he medicated himself before each show with a mind-boggling combination of five Dexedrines and ten milligrams of Thorazine ("as balance and check"). The effect was, as he observed later, "chaos in search of frenzy." Finally, he let his drug-induced stream-of-consciousness rambling go a little too far: "Now that Marilyn Monroe is kosher," he casually remarked on the day after playwright Arthur Miller and Monroe were remarried by a rabbi, "Arthur Miller can eat her." Though Levant protested that he hadn't meant it "that way," he was thrown off the air the same day. Later he blamed his perverse subconscious for tricking him into saying something so outrageous that it was bound to get him thrown off the air. (It worked.)

Saying he'd been deeply wounded by the show's cancellation, Levant suffered another breakdown that required him to be hospitalized. Several months later, he returned to his show, more manic than ever, and full of hilarious anecdotes about his stay in the funny farm. But it wasn't long before he (or his subconscious) once again went too far with some indelicate remarks about Mae West's sex life. The gaffe convinced the station that it was time for Levant to be taped—a decision that even Levant concurred with: "I found myself saying outrageous things that not only frightened me, but the whole community." But, of course, taping eliminated the danger, and along with it the exhilaration of doing the broadcast. Levant decided the fun was over and soon after left the show. Declining guest shots on talk and variety shows, he once again disappeared from public life to devote full time to his inner demons. This time it was for good.

The Smothers Brothers had a press conference to discuss CBS's cancellation of their weekly comedy-variety show.

It was the year of LSD, protests, and the Summer of Love, but television was still mired in corny clichés back at the Ponderosa ranch, and Alan King was the country's idea of an outrageous comedian when *The Smothers Brothers Comedy Hour* first took to the airwaves in 1967. By simply acknowledging the country's shifting demographics and directing itself to the massive baby boom generation by using rock music and irreverent humor, the Smothers' show tapped into a sensibility that no one else on network TV had acknowledged—let alone exploited.

The show was an immediate ratings winner, a solid moneymaker, which apparently gave the Smothers the idea that they could do as they pleased. Silly boys. Not that they were so *very* outrageous: Their politics—left-wing, and increasingly opposed to the war in Vietnam—were shared by much of the nation's young. And so was their manner—smug, self-righteous, and hipper-than-thou. No, all that they could get away with. It was messing around with God that got them in real trouble.

When God made a guest appearance in a sketch, the nation's clergy became so enraged that Tom and Dick were forced to do an on-the-air apology. From that point on, the network saw to it that the censor's pencil was wielded with much more vigor. But the Smothers continued to stick it to the network. An Elaine May sketch mocked the situation by having a censor change a line that read "My heart beats wildly in my breast whenever you are near," to "My pulse beats loudly in my wrist whenever you are near." And the long-blacklisted folk singer Pete Seeger lived up to his reputation by singing "Waist Deep in the Big Muddy," a not-so-subtle diatribe against the war and LBJ.

As the show's sentiments became more pointed, taking aim not only at the Vietnam War and the silent majority but at motherhood and the police, the network began to insist that the shows be completed early enough in the week so that they could be screened by its affiliates and censors for any offensive material. The brothers and their writers—Steve Martin, Chevy Chase, Elaine May, and Bob Einstein, among others—like the naughty children they were, repeatedly balked at delivering the shows early. Finally, in the spring of 1969, after months of bitter contention, the brothers refused to release a tape to the network, and in so doing so exasperated CBS president Robert Wood that he pulled the plug on the series.

Despite rumblings about infringements of the First Amendment and such, the Smothers had been successfully silenced. The show was picked up by ABC a year later, but by then it was too late: The Smothers Brothers' moment was over.

In 1974, a naked man streaked past David Niven during a presentation on the Academy Awards telecast. Rumor had it, though, that the whole thing was a setup, as was David Niven's "ad-lib" in which he chided the streaker for "showing off his shortcomings."

151

152

Ed Sullivan had been highly critical of Elvis Presley at the beginning of his meteoric rise to stardom, declaring him "unfit for family viewing." In so saying, he was simply echoing the public condemnation of Presley that was building in many quarters. An Elvis effigy had been hung in Nashville and another burned in St. Louis. And the real Elvis's lower-body movements had been banned in the entire state of Florida.

But it wasn't long before Elvis had become the biggest act in the country, and that meant that Sullivan, as America's premier showman, would have to swallow his objections and land him for his Sunday night show, particularly in light of the fact that Presley had recently created a sensation with Sullivan's NBC rival, Steve Allen. Instead of paying the $5,000 Colonel Tom Parker had asked for originally, Sullivan now had to cough up $50,000 for a three-performance deal.

By the time the third and final date rolled around, Presley was a superstar, and while he could easily have bought his way out of the contract with Sullivan, he and the Colonel honored their commitment and settled on a date. They made only one stipulation: that Elvis be televised from Hollywood, where he was making his first motion picture, and his performance integrated into the show. This posed a hair-raising problem for Sullivan, since he wasn't certain that AT&T and the CBS engineers could reverse the east-west transcontinental cable broadcast on cue. That left him faced with the possibility that, after a tremendous buildup, he might introduce Elvis live from Hollywood only to come up with nothing but an empty screen. Moreover, Sullivan's staff had to handle his few minutes on air like a two-hour special, taking over the largest CBS studio available and arranging for a full complement of engineers, cameramen, sets, and props. Police cordons were set up inside and outside CBS's West Coast headquarters, and special security guards were posted around his dressing room to protect him from hysterical fans.

Then, to add to the overall insanity, one of Sullivan's flunkies panicked him on the day before the show by telling him that Elvis had lately taken to performing obscene stunts in concert. According to Sullivan's producer, Marlo Lewis, Sullivan came to him with a story that had Elvis pulling a stunt at his concerts that involved, in his words, "hanging a small soft drink bottle from his groin underneath his pants so that when he wiggles his leg it looks like his pecker reaches down to his knees." "Why not just tell the Colonel to stop him?" Lewis asked. "Are you kidding?" Sullivan replied. "If it was that easy, I wouldn't be worried. But we can't tell him anything at this point. I don't think the Colonel can either. His Royal Highness is gonna do what His Royal Highness wants to do."

Sullivan dispatched Lewis to California to make sure that there weren't any slip-ups. And while Lewis saw no sign that Elvis meant to try anything cute, what he did see during run-throughs unnerved him. "Presley's movements had become so explicitly sexual, so frenziedly phallic, that, bottle or no bottle, I knew we couldn't photograph him in full torso." Lewis's trepidation led to the legendary performance that showed Presley only from the waist up.

This is just so much self-aggrandizing hooey on Lewis's part, according to one of Presley's biographers, Albert Goldman, who maintains that far from being an act of censorship, Elvis's truncated performance was a deliberate tease contrived by a master showman to titillate viewers into believing that something wild was going on "down there" out of range of the camera.

Another great bowdlerized TV moment has taken on more legendary dimensions in the retelling than it ever could have had in the viewing: In 1983, a lavish Motown twenty-fifth anniversary special featuring dozens of stars, including Michael Jackson and Smokey Robinson, was to climax with the reunion of the Supremes. But the reunion very nearly became a free-for-all as Diana Ross—who had never stopped in the name of love or anything else when it came to trampling over the other Supremes to grab the spotlight—attempted to reclaim her status as the sublime Supreme by moving front and center of her sister Supremes Mary Wilson and Cindy Birdsong. In the past, the two women had maintained a respectful distance, but for this spectacular event, they decided to stand up to Ross by taking their positions by her side. And so, as Ross stepped forward, they too stepped forward. On the defensive, Ross, who'd seemed lost and disoriented right from her showy entrance, appeared to become even more distracted during the resulting minuet, thus affording Wilson a chance to take over the lead solo on "Some Day We'll Be Together."

In an attempt to save the rapidly disintegrating scene, Smokey Robinson, Richard Pryor, and Billy Dee Williams were dispatched to join the group on stage. On a roll by this point, Mary Wilson called out to Motown boss Berry Gordy in the audience, "Berry, come on down," thereby invoking Ross's wrath since Ross had apparently wanted it to look like she'd issued the invitation. "Diana suddenly turned and pushed me," Mary Wilson said afterward. "The next thing I knew, she forced my left hand down, pushing the microphone away from my mouth. Looking me right in the eyes, she said loudly, 'It's been taken care of!' The audience gasped. In a flash I saw something in her eyes that told me she knew she'd crossed the line." Wilson went on to say that, "In earlier days, Diana would often do things like this, but never in public. . . . Of course, on the tape all you see is Diana turning around and calling out to Berry."

Although the editing of the resulting TV special made Diana come out the very picture of baby love, sisterly love, and every other kind of love, the incident was widely reported over the next few days and elaborated upon in several biographies. It was, in many ways, a turning point in Ross's career, marking the end of her reign as a media darling and the beginning of her image as a shrewish and sometimes batty prima donna.

In 1959 *Playhouse 90* televised the riveting drama "Judgment at Nuremberg," which dealt with the Nazi war crimes trials and the extermination of six million Jews in gas chambers. But one of the show's sponsors happened to be the Gas Industry of America, and because this was an era when sponsors still could exert significant influence on the content of a telecast, all references to the gas chambers were blipped, leaving confused viewers to wonder what characters were talking about when they said, "Millions were led to the —"

The National Rifle Association convinced advertisers to remove commercials from a CBS documentary called *The Guns of Autumn*, which made a strong statement for gun control.

VIDEO À CLEF

Both the mainstream and tabloid press had a field day with the story of Bryant Gumbel's purloined memo and the star-studded off-screen brawl it sparked. But nowhere did it receive more delicious coverage than on *Murphy Brown,* when a memo of Murphy's complaining about her co-workers' faults also happened to fall into the wrong hands. What with Murphy being the grouch she is, the set-up would have worked on its own terms, even without the additional fillip of its allusions to reality; but it was even funnier with them, because we—the huge television family—were sharing an inside joke with our friends in the box.

As close as they get, even scandal sheets can't always give us the real lowdown on the public personalities who capture our imagination—at least not until death or documented court proceedings reduce the threat of libel suits. But dramatic license (or in the case of *Murphy Brown,* sitcom license) allows mischief-makers like *Murphy's* creator Diane English to revel in these headline-making stories while they're still hot—taking them to whatever outlandish reaches their febrile minds can envision. Like the movies, television has been changing the names to protect the innocent and nail the naughty for years. Of course, the distinction between the two has been known to get a bit blurry in the process, if not turned completely inside out.

Rod Serling's adaptation of "The Comedian" for *Playhouse 90* took as its inspiration a cuddly TV star who became a monster when the cameras weren't rolling. The loud-mouthed funnyman who tormented those closest to him while desperately seeking the public's love couldn't possibly have been anyone but Mr. Television himself, Uncle Miltie—or so TV audiences thought back in 1957. But as it turned out, "The Comedian" also drew heavily upon the prison camp atmosphere that existed behind-the-scenes at another well-known TV comic's show.

On a somewhat more somber note, television has even managed to parlay this device into a long-running series. *The Fugitive* converted one of the hottest crime stories of the day—the trial of accused wife-killer Dr. Sam Sheppard—into a soap opera that was so compelling that it ended up obscuring the facts of the real-life case and perhaps even influencing its outcome.

The use of a recognizable character, even in a minor role, can create an almost subliminal suggestion of gritty realism that is very appealing to audiences. When *Lou Grant* patterned its feisty Margaret Pynchon character on *Washington Post* owner Katharine Graham, it wasn't so much to provide us with dirt on Graham as to lend an air of further authenticity to an already hard-hitting show.

On the other hand, we don't always recognize the real-life inspirations for some of our favorite characters—unless by some unlikely concatenation of circumstances their own fame happens to eclipse that of their TV alter egos. Norman Lear made no secret of the fact that he had based Maude, the ballsy sitcom housewife, on his own wife of many years; but that fact didn't really hit home with viewers until his ballsy wife, Frances, hit him with a mega-buck divorce suit and struck out very showily on her own. And while it's easy now to see the similarities between Carl Reiner and comedy writer Rob Petrie on *The Dick Van Dyke Show,* most of us didn't make the connection at the time—perhaps because Reiner confused matters by playing a caricatured version of his old *Your Show of Shows* boss, Sid Caesar, rather than assuming his real-life role as the writer.

In yet another conceit borrowed from the movies, celebrities are occasionally induced to play TV roles that flirt with their own splashy private lives and then flout the truth in the spirit of high camp. These might be cameo appearances that allow a casting director the indulgence of a witty aside—as when *Miami Vice* preferred Watergate loony G. Gordon Liddy as an ex-commander in Vietnam who used his warped code of honor to pursue his own immoral aims back in the States. Such subtle riffs are sometimes expanded to a full-blown plot point—as when ex–Miss America Vanessa Williams, dethroned for posing for raunchy S & M pinups, played a call girl who blackmailed Johns with incriminating bondage videotapes in her

155

first TV movie, *The Sex Tapes*. (Sure, it was compromising stuff, but it's not as if Vanessa were getting offers from *Highway to Heaven* at the time.) This gambit can sometimes pack a double wallop—say, for instance, if a star is too young to understand the exploitative nature of this particular kind of self-revelation, as when fourteen-year-old Drew Barrymore, herself an outpatient from a drug rehab center, starred in the TV movie *15 and Getting Straight*.

Audiences are particularly titillated by the idea of watching real-life couples play what gives every indication of being themselves—as with the gloriously mismatched husband-and-wife team of Jill Eikenberry and Michael Tucker on *L.A. Law*. But sometimes this kind of stunting can backfire, when off-screen hostility oozes into public view and undermines the fantasy so carefully conjured up on the tube. Lucy and Desi, Sonny and Cher, and Jim and Tammy are a few of the loving couples whose video destinies were capsized by their stormy private lives.

Despite the potential boomerang effect, actors continue to play along, pandering to the public's fascination with the interplay between real life and TV fiction. Prissy, nitpicking Tony Randall plays prissy, nitpicking Felix Unger, and professional dad Bill Cosby crafts sitcom fantasy around his celebrated rapport with kids, just as Danny Thomas had done before him (though both of their shows were less an extension of their own home lives than of their stand-up routines).

Television's intimate nature and innate tackiness have enabled us to take part in the birth of Lucy and Desi's son; to play matchmaker for Sonny and Cher after their bitter divorce; to act as a support group for Delta Burke (and Suzanne Sugarbaker) when she (they) confronted a hefty weight problem; and to hang out at home with stars like Ozzie and Harriet and Donna and Bing—who were just like the people they played. . . .

Well, weren't they?

Let's find out.

CBS was not at all pleased to discover that the star of *I Love Lucy* was expecting. It wasn't as if the pregnancy could be incorporated into the action of the show. For one thing, it was 1952 and the P-word was strictly taboo on the air. And then there were the sordid implications of such a situation—Lucy and

Lucy on the set with her "Million Dollar Baby," **Desi Arnaz, Jr.**

Ricky clearly had not been spending all their time in those cute little twin beds. The advertising agency handling *Lucy*'s sponsor, Philip Morris, helpfully suggested that Lucy conceal her condition by wearing baggy clothes and hiding behind potted plants—better yet, that she be completely written out of the show during the last few months of her term.

But all such options went out the window once Louella Parsons broke the news in her column. Lucy—along with many of her fans—fretted that the pregnancy would mean the cancellation of the series, then going into its second season. But Desi Arnaz, the father of both the TV and real-life babies, mounted a campaign aimed at convincing Alfred Lyons, the head of Morris, that the birth would be a publicity bonanza. Lyons eventually relented and wired network and agency principals: "Don't fuck around with the Cuban." Ultimately, the facts of life were cunningly interwoven with TV fantasy and the Arnazes exploited the blessed event for all it was worth.

Forty-four million people were on hand for Little Ricky's filmed birth on January 19, 1953. With impeccable timing, Lucy produced Desi Arnaz, Jr., the same night. (Because the birth was to be performed by cesarean section, Lucy's doctors were able to time it to coincide with the broadcast.) The next day people could talk of nothing else. The story made headlines in every newspaper in the country, even managing to edge out coverage of the inauguration of President Eisenhower. National magazines clamored for photos of the new baby. (In what could come to be seen as a symbolic gesture, Arnaz bypassed major magazines like *Life* and *Look* and gave the first photos of the baby to a publication called *TV Guide,* which was also just starting out in life.) A million telegrams, letters, and baby presents were delivered to the show, and a single record cut by Desi called "There's a Brand New Baby at Our House" made the Top Ten. The tumult underscored as never before the family feeling viewers had for this new brand of celebrity—the TV star.

Americans watched with parental pride as Little Ricky (child actor Richard Keith) grew up to be a conga-playing, bow-tied miniature of his TV dad—many taking him to be the Arnazes' real son. Alas, the confusion extended to Desi, Jr., too, who for years suffered an intense case of sibling rivalry with his TV brother.

Years after the publicity bonanza surrounding the matching births of Little Ricky and Desi, Jr., producer Gary Goldberg incorporated Meredith Baxter-Birney's real-life pregnancy into the storyline of *Family Ties* with similarly happy results—a new character for the show (Andrew Keaton), and a temporary shift of attention from Michael J. Fox back to Baxter-Birney, the show's intended star.

Bill Cosby, on the other hand, nixed the idea of having the stork stop off at the Huxtables' on his way

from Phylicia Rashad's. (Not that Coz doesn't like children, you understand; he was simply concerned about upsetting the show's delicate balance—a balance conservatively estimated to be worth about a half-billion dollars in syndication royalties alone.)

Cindy Williams's pregnancy (by comedian Bill Hudson) led to her departure from the long-running hit *Laverne and Shirley*—or so she later claimed. In truth, there had been friction between Williams and her co-star, Penny Marshall, right from the beginning, with Williams constantly jockeying for position so as to compensate for any possible favoritism shown her co-star by producer-director Garry Marshall—who, as everyone on the planet must know by now, is Penny's brother. And then too, there was the general pressure of the series grind on Williams, who was used to the more civilized pace of moviemaking. "It's the most brutal work I've done since working the midnight shift at the House of Pancakes," she complained.

In an effort to appease Williams, the pregnancy was incorporated into the action as "Mrs. Shirley Feeney Meany" announced a "teeny weeny Meany." But when Williams demanded that the producers limit her hours on the set, the producers helpfully suggested that she simply not be included in every episode, which would not only make life easier for her but save them $75,000 per show. "What they really want to do," Williams said, "is to ace me out of the show and finally give it all to Penny." While Mrs. Shirley Feeney Meany took a surprise trip overseas to be with her medic husband, Williams took a trip to civil court to file a $20 million lawsuit against Paramount for contract violations and discrimination. In the interim, Marshall tried to carry *Laverne and Shirley* on her own, but the fantasy floundered without the interplay between the two "best friends" and soon went off the air.

When Cybill Shepherd happened to become pregnant during *Moonlighting*'s third season, some insiders whispered that it was a last-ditch attempt to get out of her contract. No such luck. *Moonlighting*'s producer-creator Glenn Gordon Caron opted to write the pregnancy into the show—even though he appeared to take it as a personal affront. Unfortunately, there was no way to balance Maddie's delicate condition with the romantic tension that had animated David and Maddie's sexually charged repartee. "I think *Moonlighting* ended in the episode where they slept together," Willis said later. "For what the show originally was, was them not fucking. As soon as they did that, we knew it would change. It just died a little death then."

Unlike real life, in which Cybill gave birth to twins, Maddie lost her baby, in an embarrassingly dumb season-opening episode. From there the show grew progressively mushy—that is, when it wasn't being stupidly slapshticky. After a few more lame attempts to recharge the old David-and-Maddie chemistry, *Moonlighting* was put out of its misery—with Caron assigning much of the blame for the show's downfall on Cybill and her pregnancy. "I think it's important to deal with the sexism of that remark," Cybill responded. "In the Middle Ages, I'd probably be labeled a witch."

The credits said it all:
"Ozzie" . . . . Ozzie Nelson
"Harriet" . . . . Harriet Nelson
"David" . . . . David Nelson
"Ricky" . . . . Ricky Nelson

The Adventures of Ozzie and Harriet was not only a carryover of the Nelson family's successful radio show, but of their own wholesome life. Or so we were meant to believe.

But revisionist history in the form of a lurid biography of Rick Nelson has subverted the blissful picture of the gentle, low-keyed couple who asked little more of life than to watch their boys grow up. There, Harriet—who never seemed to get out of the kitchen—is said never to have been inside one (which would make sense given that she was a busy TV star, wife, and mother). And Ozzie—who had no apparent job other than mowing the lawn or raking leaves—is revealed to be a savvy businessman; a producer, actor, and exec. Contrary to being perplexed by his son's singing career, as he played it on the show, it was he who engineered Rick's bid for teen-idol stardom, leveraging his money and connections to get him recorded and then force-feeding his records to millions of viewers by way of a performance tag at the end of each weekly episode. None of that is terribly shocking to hard-core fans. More unsettling, however, is the image of Rick growing up to be an Elvis-style rock 'n' roll recluse.

Mr. Adams and Eve must have seemed like a good idea at the time—coming as it did after the stunning TV success of that other married show-

business couple. But Ida Lupino and Howard Duff were no match for Lucy and Desi.

Unlike Ball, Ida Lupino didn't attempt to pass herself off as a blithely blithering housewife. On the contrary, she came across on the tube very much the same way she did in real life—as a tough actress who was nobody's fool. Duff, on the other hand, seemed affable but a bit wishy-washy, the kind of man who might let his more powerful movie-star wife call the shots. Moreover, the Adamses didn't have any adorable little tykes running around the house, so there was little household hilarity to milk. Instead, *Mr. Adams and Eve* captured what may have been a bit too much of the Duffs' real-life problems, including business hassles and occasional behind-the-scenes strain on the marriage—grown-up concerns which went completely against the grain of the infantilized, family-oriented sitcoms of the fifties.

Neither the series nor the marriage was destined to last. Too bad.

159

Even though Carl Reiner was reasonably well known from his days with *Your Show of Shows,* the fact that he had modeled the Petrie family of *The Dick Van Dyke Show* on his own didn't really come into focus until many years later, after we'd become better acquainted with Reiner's real-life son, Rob, courtesy of a quite different TV family.

Reiner would end up playing the tyrannical Alan Brady—who, it's easy to see now, was an overdrawn version of Sid Caesar, Reiner's old boss on *Your Show of Shows.* Although much sweeter than Brady, Caesar was known to rule his show with an iron fist, presiding over writers' meetings from a golden throne. (Literally.)

Mickey Rooney and Mel Torme in The Comedian.

Milton Berle makes like Orson Welles.

Red Buttons shows one of his writers how to do it right.

Milton Berle was notorious for being an incorrigible scene stealer and joke thief, not to mention a control freak who told directors how to direct and lighting men how to light. So when *Playhouse 90*'s Rod Serling did an adaptation of novelist Ernest Lehman's portrait of a vicious, greedy, selfish, lecherous, all-round son-of-a-bitch TV star, the buzz was, not surprisingly, that "The Comedian" was in reality none other than Mr. Television himself.

Actually, Berle had taken even deadlier aim at himself right at the height of his TV popularity in the movie *Always Leave Them Laughing* (1949), in which he played an uproarious but obnoxious joke-stealing comic. And besides, he was a pussycat compared to Serling's other probable source of inspiration—Red Buttons. The diminutive, cuddly Buttons bullied and browbeat a string of writers and staff people during the early run of his TV show, becoming increasingly abusive as the show's popularity waned. After two years of frantic tinkering following a move from CBS to NBC, *The Red Buttons Show* was cancelled (1955). Although Buttons didn't know it at the time, he would never again have a weekly niche in TV.

By this point, Berle too had become a shadow of his former, wildly successful self. After his show was cancelled in 1956, he descended into a funk that was relieved only through the help of his Christian Science practitioner. Not that he was tapped—anything but. At the height of Berlemania, he'd signed a twenty-five-year pay-or-play contract giving him enough money to keep him in cigars and Caddies until 1974. But NBC seemed to want him only for hosting chores on *The Kraft Music Hall* and *Jackpot Bowling*—quite a comedown for Mr. Television. In between, he worked Vegas and the Borscht Belt, doing the usual roasts, toasts, and eulogies. It was a cushy situation—for anyone, that is, who didn't crave public love as desperately as Uncle Miltie.

Elvis on the set of King Creole with director Michael Curtis and producer Hal Wallis.

161

Never one to miss a chance to merchandise his boy, Colonel Tom Parker made a deal with NBC to do a live TV drama that would parallel Elvis Presley's sudden rise to fame—and star him as well. But by the time the network got around to it in 1956, Elvis was a huge star, too huge to bother with some dinky little TV role. His anxiously-awaited film debut in *Love Me Tender* was scheduled for later that same year.

To fill in for Elvis, the Colonel summoned a young singer he'd managed a few years earlier, Tommy Sands. Sands was a sensation in the role; and "Teen-age Crush," one of the show's featured songs, became a huge hit. In a matter of weeks his own rise to stardom would imitate TV (which was already imitating life) as he became one of Elvis's designated heirs apparent—though it should have been obvious to all that no one, least of all Tommy, could ever replace the King.

Tommy Sands in The Singing Idol.

162

Carl Reiner modeled *The Dick Van Dyke Show*'s
husband-hunting comedy writer Sally Rogers (originally "Sally Diamond") on two women he had
worked with on *Your Show of Shows,* Lucille Kallen
and Selma Diamond. Sally's resemblance to Diamond was particularly obvious, and probably inten-
tionally so, since Diamond was by that point
something of a celebrity herself by way of frequent
appearances on *The Tonight Show.* Her stock shtick
there consisted of complaining, in her unmistakable
parched, nasal whine, about her supposedly bleak
personal life. ("And where will you be appearing
next?" Johnny Carson once asked her in his ritual
end-of-show query. "In the laundromat," she dead-
panned. "I figure my towels should be dry by now.")

Diamond's habit of canvassing the *Tonight Show*
audience for single men found its way into a 1966
episode called "Dear Sally Rogers," which showed
Sally advertising for a husband on "The Stevie Parsons Show."

The sensational murder trial of Dr. Sam Sheppard, an Ohio osteopath who was accused of bludgeoning his pregnant wife to death, was dragging into its eighth year on appeal when Dr. Richard Kimble was sentenced to death for the murder of his wife on the debut episode of *The Fugitive.* Like Sheppard, Kimble claimed to have seen the real culprit—in this case a one-armed man—fleeing the scene of the crime. But unlike Sheppard, Kimble was able to escape the authorities and set off in hot pursuit of the villain. For the duration of the highly successful series, we saw him criss-crossing the country, slipping in and out 'of various odd jobs and identities, while also taking time out to do good deeds—sort of a Mary Worth on the lam.

In a remarkable two-episode climax to the series' fourth and final season, the second of which garnered a whopping 72 percent share of the TV audience, *The Fugitive* brought its hero's quest to a successful conclusion, when Kimble finally tracked the real killer down, and exonerated himself of his wife's murder.

In real life, the Supreme Court threw out Sheppard's 1954 conviction during the third year of *The Fugitive*'s run, citing the prejudicial effect of the ''virulent publicity'' attending the case.

163

''Maude Starts a Magazine'': In this laugh-filled episode, the irrepressible Maude divorces her husband, Walter Findley, and takes $30 million of her $112 million alimony settlement to start a women's magazine. Convinced she can use herself as a barometer for all women's tastes (just as Walter had used her as the model for a beloved sitcom character who, like her, was a well-to-do housewife who dabbled in liberal politics), Maude creates a magazine ''for the woman who was born a loooooong time ago.'' She calls it *Findley's* despite the fact that she despises Walter. Not one to let a little thing like not knowing anything about the magazine business cramp her style, Maude presides over *Findley's* staff meetings robed in satin and attended by her retinue of cook, butler, masseuse, personal trainer, and psychologist. After hiring several editors, picking their brains, and then abruptly dismissing them, Maude sees her magazine become a smashing success—making her husband's name even more famous than it was before their messy divorce. (30 min.)

Saccharine and implausible as it was, the concept that provided the basis for *The Partridge Family* —a wholesome family rock group that toured the country in a brightly painted school bus—didn't originate with some wash-'n'-wear TV exec but with a real-life rock band—the Cowsills.

The Beatle-ish group had several hits in the late 60s (until their squeaky-clean image became a liability). In fact, the family was supposed to play itself until the network insisted on Shirley Jones playing their mother, scratching the deal. The Cowsills were eventually eclipsed by their TV counterparts, who scored several hits ("I Think I Love You," etc.) and produced their very own monster star, David Cassidy —whose career has never recovered from the oppressive Partridge Family hype.

164

The Cowsills

The Partridges

The Loud family (Bill and Pat Loud and their three sons and daughter) were as natural as could be expected while being tracked through their Santa Barbara house by PBS documentary cameras for three months. Much of the familial interplay was as humdrum as that of any family, but the filmmakers' tenacity paid off when they captured middle son Lance announcing his gayness and father Bill informing his wife that he was leaving.

Intrigued by *An American Family,* producer Leonard Goldberg fashioned a weekly drama series called *Family* about a contemporary clan facing the same difficult problems as those plaguing the Louds, as opposed to the pimples and proms that were the stuff of drama for *The Brady Bunch.*

The Louds

The Lawrences

The Reagans

Still smarting from the recession years of the Carter presidency, America was ready to wake up to champagne kisses and caviar dreams by the time the 1980 presidential election rolled around. Ronald Reagan's landslide victory sent the message that good ol' boys were out and glitz was in. One of the first to get the message, soap opera queen Esther Shapiro exploited the new let-them-eat-cake sensibility by unveiling a new prime time family saga of unscrupulous power players. She called it *Dynasty*. As the models for her own filthy-rich first couple, Blake and Krystle, Shapiro chose the country's most conspicuous consumers—Ronnie and Nancy.

Dynasty's popularity mirrored the President's during the early eighties but it slipped dramatically in 1988 along with the stock market and Ollie North's reputation. By 1989, both Reagan and *Dynasty* had been cancelled and the typical TV family had returned to stark reality in a blue-collar bungalow with Roseanne Barr.

The Carringtons

After all those years in authority at the WJM newsroom, benignly bossing around compliant females like Mary Richards, it must have been a shock for the churlish Lou Grant to square off with his willful new female boss at the *Los Angeles Tribune*, Margaret Pynchon. Pynchon (Nancy Marchand) had inherited the paper from her husband and ran it with steely determination—just like another widowed newspaper publisher, the feisty owner of the *Washington Post* (whose name became a household word during the Watergate scandal), Katharine Graham.

With a bow to the hip TV-savvy style of the movie *Broadcast News* and the old *Mary Tyler Moore Show,* Diane English played on the public's familiarity with the inner workings of TV news to create Murphy Brown, a scrappy TV reporter with the blond-goddess looks of Diane Sawyer and the orneriness of Linda Ellerbee. (English even got the real Ellerbee to play herself on a show in which Murphy challenged her for the credit of coining "And so it goes.")

In addition to Ellerbee, various other CBS news stars showed up over the course of the show's first year. And while Bryant Gumbel didn't appear on the show, his infamous memo did when a high-school hacker lifted a vitriolic critique of her co-workers from Murphy's computer. (Unlike Gumbel, Murphy didn't have to apologize to her colleagues on the air.) Next, a Jane Pauley/Deborah Norville–style coup d'état was narrowly averted when Corky, Murphy's young and ambitious co-star, beat Murphy out of an Emmy. Corky got her comeuppance when she had to beg for Murphy's help on a story far over her own perfectly coiffed head. In case anyone might have missed the allusions, English had Corky exclaim upon hearing of her Emmy nomination, "And to think I was afraid my looks would keep me from getting the kind of recognition I deserve!"—a not-so-subtle echo of Norville's lament that being stone gorgeous had made it difficult for her to be taken seriously.

Just like **Barbara Mandrell**: **Oral** and friends sell God and glitz.

167

Glory, Glory's singing soul-sister Ruth wasn't Tammy and she wasn't Jimmy and she wasn't Oral exactly—but the creators of this HBO four-parter didn't mind if you made the associations. Heck, they practically guaranteed you would. And why shouldn't they? After all, *Glory*'s producer, Bonny Dore, had at one time worked with none other than Oral "If-you-don't-send-me-$100-the-Lord-is-gonna-call-me-home" Roberts, who'd hired her to add a little pizazz to his prime-time TV show after seeing what she'd done for Barbara Mandrell. "A lot of stuff in the [*Glory*] script came right out of those days," Dore observed pointedly.

But apparently, the life-styles of the rich and self-righteous were too raunchy even for pay cable. Yup, next to the tabloid revelations about Tammy's K-Mart habit, Jim and Jessica's first date, and Jimmy Swaggart's leisure-time activities, Sister Ruth's addictions (primarily cocaine and spandex) seemed downright tame.

168

Well, hot dang, that cotton-candy-haired, country gal singer in the made-for-TV movie *Country Gold* sure looks familiar. Wonder who she's supposed to be? Loni Anderson was poured into fancy rodeo-style togs just like the Porter Wagoner–era Dolly Parton, but the problems she had with balancing her stardom and her personal life were more on the order of those faced by Loretta Lynn in *Coal Miner's Daughter.*

During the years he starred as Caine, *Kung Fu*'s Zen cowboy, David Carradine was living the trendy life of a Tinseltown bohemian. One of Hollywood's most flamboyant hippies, he and his then-wife Barbara Seagull (née Hershey) had gone "back to nature" in a tumble-down house in the hills overlooking L.A. There Carradine gave interviews espousing the Caine philosophy of patience, peace, and killing only when absolutely necessary (i.e., when the ratings were slipping). "I forgot I was a kid born in Hollywood who likes to ride horses and drive fast cars. Instead I became absorbed by my character. I was this guy who walks around barefoot and won't ride a horse because he doesn't want to be a burden to it."

Carradine's pretensions dovetailed neatly into those of the show (a horse opera gussied up with New Age jargon), generating a great deal of the publicity that fueled its early success. But then, in 1974, during *Kung Fu*'s third season, Carradine took the crazy hippie act too far. While tripping on peyote, he broke into a neighbor's house and then wandered off through the neighborhood naked and bleeding. A subsequent lawsuit brought by a woman who claimed to have been attacked by Carradine during this rampage cast him in a very un-Grasshopperly light.

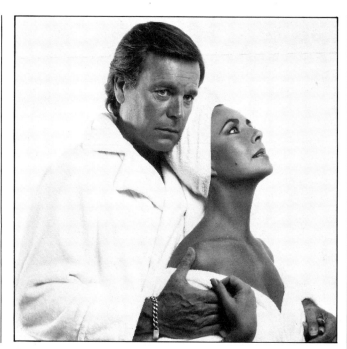

Robert Wagner and **Elizabeth Taylor** in There Must Be a Pony.

170

It could've come straight out of the pages of the *Enquirer*—the Tennessee Williams story of the fading movie queen who seeks solace in drugs, alcohol, and pretty young men. And as fate would have it, a romantic liaison between Elizabeth Taylor and a hunky young ex–truck driver was generating just such breathless tabloid headlines in the fall of 1989 when she starred in the made-for-TV movie version of *Sweet Bird of Youth.*

Of course, this wasn't the first time Liz had allowed her own life to be used as grist for the cinematic exploitation mill. The phenomenon had begun in 1950 when MGM exploited her nuptials to hotel heir Nicky Hilton with *Father of the Bride.* And in the early sixties, she'd graciously pandered to the public's curiosity about her scandalous love affair with Richard Burton by acting it out in soapy romances like *The Sandpiper* and *The VIPs.* In later years, Our Liz even lampooned her own bigger-than-life star status in *The Mirror Crack'd.* Such candor seemed perfectly natural coming from a star who was so much a part of the nation's family as Our Liz.

When her box-office drawing power began to fade, Liz continued her ongoing autobiography on the small screen, where she played an actress recovering from a painful breakdown in *There Must Be a Pony* following her first, much-publicized treatment for al-

cohol and drug abuse at the Betty Ford Clinic in 1983. It was during Liz's second sojourn in rehab that she took up with the young trucker who was to give her romantic interludes with Mark Harmon a special spin in *Sweet Bird of Youth.*

Taylor had been producer Linda Yellen's first, and only, choice for the role—even though her chronic back problems cost the production several problematic delays. "With Elizabeth Taylor in the part [of the Princess]," observed Yellen, "the piece keeps moving from fiction to reality. The Princess's line 'By the time I was thirty-one, I was a living legend' takes on a special resonance when a real legend says it."

Debby Harry as rock star Diana Price on Wiseguy.

In a 1989 episode of *Wiseguy*, Ken Wahl, as Vinnie Terranova, lavished a truckload of OCB money on a record that he hoped would resurrect the career and self-respect of Diana Price, a former rock queen coming off a bad decade. And who could blame him? After all, playing Diana was the luscious Debbie Harry —a former rock queen who herself happened to be coming off a down period. Happily, Harry's appearance marked what has turned out to be a successful comeback to both recording and acting.

Why pussyfoot around the facts in a disguised rendering of the story of your life, why play it coy, when you can act out your own more flattering version of the way it was on TV? In the "Me, Wonderful Me" style video biography, the stars play themselves.

Imagine being able to share Shirley MacLaine's search for inner peace (not to mention getting the deep dish on her torrid affair with a married man) in a five-hour, two-part made-for-TV movie *Out on a Limb.* Of course, it had all been there in her best-selling book of the same name, but it was so much more compelling to watch Shirley actually live through it all again, to see her and some of the original, real-life participants recreate actual interludes—such as when trance channelers Sture Johanssen and Kevin Ryerson dramatized Shirley's initiation into channeling. (Were the psychics "acting" for the cameras? Or had they, in fact, been acting all along?) So what if the big-budget special effects didn't make much of a case for the supernatural? What *Out on a Limb* did inadvertently illuminate was the connection between Shirley's mystical rebirth and what gave every indication of being a severe midlife crisis—particularly in light of the fact that her magical mystery tour had taken place in the late sixties and early seventies—a rough period that saw her suffering through several lame movies (e.g., *John Goldfarb, Please Come Home*) and a failed TV series (*Shirley's World,* 1971–72) as well as an unfulfilling flirtation with Democratic politics during the '68 and '72 presidential campaigns.

While trounced by critics, *Out on a Limb* was a sensation with Shirley's millions of fans and a growth experience for Shirley—one that inspired her to write yet another book, this one about the revelations that came to her while playing herself on TV. (The obvious question now is whether there will be a TV movie based on her book about playing herself in the TV movie based on her previous book—starring Shirley, of course.)

Sophia Loren: Her Own Story posed the thought-provoking question "How can one woman be so perfect?" With Sophia in the roles of both her mother and, later, herself, this two-part made-for-TV hagiography traced the actress's climb from a poverty-stricken Rome childhood to screen-goddess maturity. Through good times and bad, Sophia exhibits the soul of a saint, often prompting the other characters to marvel at how lovely, how generous—indeed, how *perfect*—she is. What man (including the legendary Cary Grant, played by our ambassador to Mexico John Gavin) could avoid falling madly, passionately in love with such a creature? And yet in the face of unlimited romantic opportunities, Sophia remains unaccountably loyal (sort of) to her longtime husband, Carlo Ponti. Since her attraction to the pudgy producer is unexplained, viewers might guess that it had something to do with his Svengali-like manipulation of her career. Indeed, the possibility of ambition as a motivating factor in any of Sophia's life choices goes wholly unmentioned (as do those topless flicks she made as a young actress), because any suggestion to that effect might make Sophia seem less than perfect, and that would be less—far less—than what Sophia had in mind when they inflicted this mindless tale on the public.

171

172

Imagine the reaction of the Peanut Gallery (and the Peanuts' parents) had the behind-the-screen antics of the *Howdy Doody Show* cast become public knowledge. What if word had gotten out, for instance, about the notorious "blue rehearsals" at which the puppets performed certain so-called unnatural acts with each other, and both man and puppet made a practice of exposing themselves to any hapless female who crossed their paths—Chief Thunderthud by way of comedian Dayton Allen's prodigious natural endowment, and Howdy courtesy of a teeny-tiny wooden penis supplied by his zany string-pullers? As it was, the Doodyville gang came precariously close to blowing it on the air, what with Howdy's penchant for silly sexual double entendres and Princess Summerfall Winterspring (Judy Tyler) cursing like a sailor during commercial breaks.

And what would people have thought if they'd known that Father didn't always know best? That Robert Young was a tortured alcoholic prone to paralyzing depressions and volcanic fits of temper? That he was often infuriated by Billy Gray's sullen behavior and the constant on-the-set disruptions caused by Elinor ("Princess") Donahue's stage mother? That it was Jane Wyatt, with her constant peacemaking, who really knew best?

Trading off his image as a doting and prolific dad, Bing Crosby played the part of Bing Collins, a singer who had traded show business for life as a family man in *The Bing Crosby Show.* Bing spent a great deal of time mediating drippy family dilemmas, but he was never so busy he didn't have time to do a b-b-ballad every week.

Just like real life . . . huh, Gary?

Well, no.

Bing Crosby's image as a devoted dad might have endured forever were it not for the revelations made by his sons Gary, in his book, *Going My Own Way,* and Lindsay, who very pointedly took his life on Christmas Eve in 1989 after watching his Dad sing "White Christmas" in *Holiday Inn.* While exploiting his four adorable sons by a first wife, Dixie Lee, for a barrel load of publicity in the forties, Bing abused them, according to Gary, both verbally and physically, and made life miserable for their mother with his constant carousing. His relationship with his second batch of children, by actress Kathryn Grant, was apparently less turbulent—although Der Bingle seems to have conducted most of his parenting from the golf course.

173

The irrepressible, shamelessly hammy Joan Davis would do anything for a laugh—and anything to keep the upper hand on her show, the uproarious, if now dated, *I Married Joan.* Beloved in vaudeville and movies as a ditsy female clown of the Fanny Brice school, Davis off-camera was crude and frequently cruel, a despot possessed of a foul (albeit hilarious) mouth, who thought nothing of insulting a sponsor's wife or putting mice in her rodent-phobic co-star's dressing room. And yet, throughout the hit show's three-year run—indeed, for the duration of her career—Davis managed to maintain the front of a zany, lovable clown. Thanks in great part to her intense aversion to interviews, few people—even showbiz insiders—had any idea what a terror she really was, and how autocratic the rule she exercised over "the boys" (Neil Simon, Abe Burrows, and Leon Uris) who custom-tailored her comic bits of business.

The hapless Jim Backus, her underpaid, overworked co-star, felt particularly victimized by Davis: "I was an indentured servant. She owned the show and she called the shots. I was the only guy in town who came home with lipstick on his paycheck!"

174

Donna Stone was every man's dream and every woman's nightmare—a selfless, exquisitely turned-out domestic goddess, the ultimate Stepford Wife. And we all believed that she and Donna Reed, the actress who played her, were really one and the same.

The stereotyping of the former Donna Belle Mullenger as the quintessential girl-next-door had begun with her indenture to MGM and persisted through most of the thirty-five films she did in the forties and fifties. Still, her good girls had an edge, a certain bitter quality, and on occasion, a smoldering sensuality —as the love interest in *Saturday's Hero* (1951) and most notably as the prostitute, Alma, in *From Here to Eternity.* (Reed was Columbia boss Harry Cohn's personal choice for that role, although probably less because he recognized in her an untapped potential than because she was married to one of his execs.) Although she won an Academy Award for *Eternity,* she nevertheless seemed destined to languish in a

string of forgettable nice-girl roles—and never more so than when she took control of her career and made the move to TV in 1958.

How ironic, since the picture-perfect wife and mom she brought to life for TV viewers was the creation of a hard-edged businesswoman who—along with her husband, Tony Owen—owned and produced *The Donna Reed Show.* As had been the case since her studio days, the tough side of Reed's personality was softened for public consumption. And anyway, it's not as if she could have given Eisenhower America a ballsy feminist heroine. And yet the show was only in its second year when Donna began to go public with her contempt for "the two-dimensional, stereotyped woman" she played, dismissing her as "a male fantasy." But the cantankerous Donna who was beginning to emerge in interviews couldn't compete with the radiant figure who floated down the Stones' staircase and into America's homes every week.

Donna Stone was so perfect that she made women want to gag, or better yet, gag *her.* In 1966, Donna Reed finally did the job herself—exiting the show and taking her millions with her. That same year she divorced her husband and began speaking out against the Vietnam War. When both of her sons became conscientious objectors, she supported them as the chairperson of Another Mother for Peace. In later years she rallied to the support of feminist causes, vowing that if she ever returned to TV, it would be with a woman producer. "I'd never go through that ordeal again," she said of the treatment she endured under the "male mentalities who dominated TV programming"—though she did indeed return to series TV, as Miss Ellie on *Dallas,* replacing the ailing Barbara Bel Geddes. When *Dallas*'s controlling male mentalities (particularly that of Larry Hagman) cavalierly dismissed her after deciding she wasn't right for the role, she waged—and won—a typically hard-fought legal battle that earned her a million-dollar out-of-court settlement.

Okay, so Donna Stone helped foster a demeaningly idealized image of women, one that remains— thanks to a hundred hours of reruns—a symbol of Stone Age propaganda. But her off-screen life gave the lie to it. And for that we have Donna Reed to thank.

In the beginning, they'd played the part of social outcasts—hippie rebels with clothes too loud and hair too long. But by the time Sonny and Cher moved on to the greener pastures of prime time, they'd developed an act that portrayed Sonny as a dim-witted court jester and Cher as a smart, tough-talking doll who belted ballads and cut Sonny down to size with carefully scripted ad-libs. In real life, though, Sonny was the brains behind the operation and Cher, his beautiful, and talented shill.

Millions of viewers tuned in in the early 70s to watch husband and wife Sonny and Cher Bono trade barbs on *The Sonny and Cher Comedy Hour.* The repartee was fun because we knew that deep down inside, they really loved each other. And there was always the obligatory end-of-show cuddle with little Chastity Bono, their sullen offspring, in case we doubted that everything between them was warm and fuzzy.

But all was not as it seemed. As he had since their early days together, Sonny Bono kept a close rein on his young wife, screening her calls, monitoring her leisure activities, and controlling her every career move. More like a strict father than a husband, he did everything but cut her meat. At first she was grateful; after all, he had made her a star. But eventually Cher began to suspect that Sonny was more enamored of the commercial aspects of their marriage than the personal ones.

Screwing up her courage during one of their Las Vegas engagements, Cher finally escaped. But breaking up proved hard to do after CBS threatened legal action if the Bonos failed to return to their highly rated show. Grudgingly, they reunited to finish out the season. But the good times were definitely over.

The subsequent divorce was one of the messiest ever—this in a town famed for its marital morasses. It got off to a fighting start with Sonny's $24 million breach-of-contract suit against Cher. She, upon discovering that she had little, if any, share of their multimillion-dollar enterprise, countersued for "involuntary servitude."

In the fall of 1974 Sonny attempted to return to TV, but *The Sonny Comedy Review* was a dismal flop. Facing an audience alone for the first time in her life, Cher then went solo in 1975 with her own comedy-variety show on CBS. But after a strong start, her off-camera troubles—namely, her tempestuous marriage to rock star Gregg Allman—began to put a crimp in her ratings. Emitting a corporate chortle, CBS came up with the solution: In one of the more bizarre turns of a bizarre medium, they convinced Sonny and Cher to team up again. Their reunion was to be strictly professional, you understand. Conditions included (1) Sonny's dropping his lawsuit against Cher and (2) Cher's agreeing to make a personal-appearance tour with Sonny during the summer of '76.

In an attempt to acknowledge yet make light of their vastly overpublicized split, Sonny's first line to their studio audience on the debut night of their reunion show was: "Well, folks, I don't know if any of you have heard about it, but Cher and I aren't married anymore." But instead of a chuckle of recognition, there was an excruciatingly long silence, which gave way to a communal moan. If they'd been smart, they would've stopped right there—since that reaction was a preview of what was to come.

For even the most devoted Sonny and Cher lovers, the thrill was gone. The humor was forced, and the interaction between the two almost painful. In fact, with Cher a new mother by her new (and newly estranged) husband, her stock putdowns of Sonny were embarrassing, if not downright cruel. By its third airing, *The Sonny and Cher Show,* the most eagerly anticipated show of the 1976 season, had plummeted to number 38 in the ratings. After changing its time slot, CBS finally cancelled the series in the summer of 1977—mercifully killing off the weekly prime-time spectacle of Sonny and Cher once and for all.

175

PLEASE STAND BY

Pop quiz: Which of the following headlines from a recent banner edition of *The National Enquirer* constitutes a scandal?

- VANNA'S BOMBSHELL SECRET PAST REVEALED: A NIGHTMARE OF DRUGS, BEATINGS, AND WILD SEX!
- ED MCMAHON TO REUNITE WITH HIS CHEATING WIFE!
- ROSEANNE AND BOYFRIEND TOM ARNOLD HOG ELEVATOR FOR 15 STEAMY MINUTES!

Answer: None of the above.

Oh, sure, it's rough stuff—distasteful, and even demoralizing for all those involved. And yet there isn't a genuine scandal—as in "career-killing disgrace"—in the bunch. Vanna may have a secret past, but she's still turning those letters for *Wheel* fans, with nary a scarlet one in sight. Ed McMahon is still laughing it up with Johnny. And Roseanne's still hogging the ratings in her time slot.

Not that we don't care about Vanna and Ed and Roseanne. We TV-o-philes have a significant emotional investment in them as well as all the other TV stars who regularly come into our homes. More than any other celebrities, their well-being, and by extension, their private lives, are a genuine public concern.

But the relaxation of moral strictures that began in the freewheeling sixties has come to mean that such sins as drug abuse, adultery, and illegitimate children are no longer considered to be punishable by excommunication from the Church of Celebrity. By the same token, contemporary society's heightened candor about these once-taboo subjects now allows the publication of revelations that would once have been unthinkable, even during the era of Hollywood's most famous tongue-waggers, Hedda Hopper and Louella Parsons. Despite their viperish reputations, these tough old birds tended to stay away from serious dirt. Certainly, they were privy to most of the skeletons in Hollywood's walk-in closets, but, as a rule, they used their knowledge to leverage information more suitable to their breakfast-table readership, such as role castings, marriages, births, and such.

Modern-day celebrity is not for the faint-of-heart. Those who seek the spotlight in today's no-holds-barred public arena had better be prepared to take the heat, particularly in the tabloids where the temperature has never been higher. Their standard purple prose may be completely fabricated or simply slightly off-the-mark (that is, just true enough to avoid a libel suit). And then, too, it may be—and surprisingly often is—true: a compromising tidbit of information leaked by an ex-friend, disgruntled flunky, or embittered relative that has been embellished with imagined details and dialogue invented by some kamikaze tabloid scribe.

Unflattering as this kind of thing can be, it still counts as publicity, so much so that the stars occasionally conspire to create it themselves. This is accomplished by issuing candid confessionals directly to the tabloids, the more respectable supermarket slicks, or, if they're really hot, to Barbara Walters and her huge television constituency. Such frankness can end up being a solid career move, particularly if it coincides (as it did, for instance, in the case of the *People* magazine cover story "Kristy McNichol's Descent into Hell") with a comeback on a new series. There seem to be no long-term ill effects, no matter how raunchy the revelations. Short of necrophilia, there's not much we won't forgive in the way of errant behavior on the part of our stars—that is, so long as they come to us afterward to ask our forgiveness (and give us all the lurid details).

It helps to remember, though, while allowing yourself the guilty pleasure of peeking at the stars' dirty little secrets, and perhaps feeling a bit besmirched by your own prurience, that no matter what they say to the contrary, those who endure such scrutiny have usually sought it out. In fact, many of them pay astoundingly large sums of money to public relations firms to make sure that the onslaught doesn't stop. Unlike the bereaved survivors of a fire or a plane crash, the mainstays of the tabloids, the slicks, and the gossip columns typically have no desire for privacy; they welcome those marauding phalanxes of cameras and microphones that dog their every step. Certainly, they would like to control what is written about them—dictate it line by line, if possible. (And sometimes it is.) But ultimately attention is what they crave, even when it comes from *The Star* or *The National Enquirer.* Out of little more than this mutual need, celebrities are born, and then, by some curious symbiotic alchemy, taken seriously by us, their adoring public.

And so, what with wanna-bes seeking public exposure at any price, the genuine career-killing scandal threatens to go the way of the pupfish and *Hello Larry.* Gone are the days when a TV titan like Arthur Godfrey could blow his image, and ultimately his devoted following, with an on-air tantrum. Today such behavior would probably just boost his ratings. Gone, too, are the days when a debate over the ethics of television quiz shows would find its way to the floor of the Senate, and result in the cancellation of severaly highly rated shows and the near-annihilation of the genre. Of course, both of these scandals, like most of TV's juiciest, date from the 1950s when, in the words of Jackie Mason (and he should know, having been virtually banned from the air for allegedly making an obscene gesture on *The Ed Sullivan Show*): "The idea of being vocal or dirty or obscene

was ten thousand times more outrageous than now."

With the exception of those famous ad-libs by the irrepressible Dan Quayle, videotape and broadcast delays have, for the most part, rendered the career-compromising TV faux pas a thing of the past. And it's hard to imagine what it would take in the way of gossip to undermine a TV star's public image to the extent that he or she could never again be accepted on the small screen.

So what of the fate of the genuine TV scandal?

Take heart all you scandal mavens. Think of the saga of Jim and Tammy. Now *that* one had everything going for it: kinky sex, bizarro eye make-up, and God. (Grudging note: Jim-and-Tammy-mania wasn't technically a full-fledged TV scandal in that it didn't really blossom on the small screen until it showed up on *Nightline* and in Johnny Carson's monologues.)

The time has come to take a second look at a few of the great TV flaps, starting with those innocent days of the 1950s when an inane little joke could stir up a tempest in a water closet and a wayward finger could turn a career upside down.

178

Local Listings • November 1-7

TV GUIDE

15¢

WHAT THEY'RE SAYING ABOUT JACK PAAR

Jack Paar

So you think Geraldo has no shame and Morton Downey, Jr., oughta be against the law? They were nothing compared to the original, the one and only—I kid you not—Jack Paar. Paar not only invented the talk show, he patented the slavering, pandering, humble, and humbling host. He gushed, he kowtowed, he cajoled, insulted, and burst into tears—all the while holding eight million people in thrall. He made Merv look reserved; he made Dave seem sincere.

The original *Tonight Show* format—which Paar indirectly inherited from Steve Allen—revolved around comedy sketches and silly audience interaction; it was Paar's innovation to move the focus of the show to his interviews. These he conducted from behind his desk, chin cupped in his hand, leaning forward, staring raptly into the face of his prey as if they were the most fascinating people on earth. If the guests had something to say, Paar practically crawled down their throats to get it out. If they had the temerity to be boring or nonforthcoming, he was just as capable of turning his back on them and proceeding as if they didn't exist. Appearing on his show could be hazardous to a star's image, since he or she was just as likely to bomb as sparkle. Ask Mickey Rooney, who showed up tipsy one night and was informed by Paar that while he might be talented at reading other people's words in the movies, he had no business appearing on a live, unscripted show.

Paar established a rep company of talkers—Genevieve, Alexander King, Charley Weaver (Cliff Arquette), Joey Bishop, Shelley Berman, Peggy Cass, humor writer Jack Douglas, Dody Goodman—oddballs all, and, in truth, all modest talents, though each would become a household name thanks to him. The first to emerge as a star was Goodman, a former dancer with a ditsy airhead manner. Paar was wild about her, and so were his viewers. But when Goodman's popularity threatened to overtake his, he turned visibly churlish—provoking several strained exchanges. Fans took sides, and the dramatic question of Goodman's future on the show was dissected in many a newspaper squib. Not surprisingly, it was Paar who won—weaning his audience from Goodman by gradually phasing her off the show, but not before learning a valuable lesson. His viewers had, in fact, been titillated by the power struggle, he realized. As a consequence, he began to let more and more reality leak through the screen.

For his headline-making encore, Paar walked off the job in the middle of a live show. It seemed that he was miffed because NBC had deleted a mildly off-color bathroom joke from the previous night's taped broadcast. "I've been up thirty hours without an ounce of sleep," Paar announced dramatically, "wrestling with my conscience all day. I've made a decision about what I'm going to do, and only one person knows about this—Hugh Downs. My wife doesn't know, but I'll be home in time and I'll tell her. I'm leaving *The Tonight Show.* There must be a better way to make a living than this, a way of entertaining people without being constantly involved in some form of controversy. I love NBC, and they've been wonderful to me. But they let me down." With that spirited defense of freedom of speech, he bid his viewers goodbye. The studio audience went crazy, clapping and yelling for Paar's return, but the tumult was met with silence—and Hugh Downs went on to complete hosting chores on the show.

When Paar finally deigned to return a month later, the network welcomed him back with open arms. Of course, they really had no choice. You see, Paar didn't just preside over *The Tonight Show*—he *was* the show. He used his nightly ninety-minute slot as a personal soapbox from which to push his favorite people and products (a word from him could make a nobody a star or an obscure little book of gags a bestseller) and to bash his bêtes noires, which generally consisted of people, or even institutions, that didn't regard him with total reverence. When he wasn't calling Congress a "bunch of clowns" or sniping at the press, he was waging on-the-air feuds with powerful columnists like Ed Sullivan, Walter Winchell, or Dorothy Kilgallen.

Like most bullies, he was easily wounded, and he nuked anyone who dared the slightest criticism with heavy-duty artillery. For instance, when Dorothy Kilgallen chided him for his gee-whiz adoration of Fidel Castro, he viciously attacked not her politics but her chin—or lack of it. But then, aside from his beloved daughter, Randy, few women brought out the best (or even the minimally acceptable) in Paar. His favorite female guests were slightly batty dames upon whom he could heap, if not outright abuse, flagrant double entendres. For all the yelling he did about his rights, his freedom, and his integrity, Paar used the inroads he achieved to very modest ends—content to exercise his growing freedom by leering ever more openly at cleavage. (But then, what could you expect of a man whose most principled stand was taken in behalf of bathroom humor?)

179

In March of 1962, while at the height of his popularity, to the amazement of friends and foes alike, Paar decided to quit what was by then *The Jack Paar Show.* He gave no reason, save the usual one of wanting more time for his family; and to this day his sudden departure remains a mystery to most. But the truth was that he had gotten himself in hot water again, this time by documenting the presence of American soldiers at the Berlin Wall in one of his home-movie travelogues—at a time when official American policy staunchly maintained otherwise. The military muscled NBC, which then muscled Paar. Finally he had a cause worthy of his talents for drumming up publicity. But for once he kept his silence, slipping into a relatively anonymous life in Connecticut with his longtime wife, Miriam—whose multimillion-dollar inheritance from the Hershey chocolate company allowed Paar to do as he liked.

Although he attempted a return to late-night TV on ABC in 1973, the world of talking heads had long since passed him by; one by one, his competitors had one-upped him. Merv was gushier. Cavett was pithier. And Carson had invented hundreds of ways to leer at a starlet's cleavage. Who needed Jack Paar?

On the night in October of 1953 when Arthur Godfrey casually ambled over to the young Italian-American crooner Julius LaRosa after a number and said, "Thank you, Julie. And that, folks, was Julie's swan song," millions of startled viewers turned to each other and asked, "Did I just hear what I thought I heard?" Had the Old Redhead just fired his star attraction on the air—just like that? Indeed he had. No explanation, no apologies—just television history in the making.

With three network shows, Godfrey was the biggest thing in television at the time, so the incident made headlines all over the country. The story had all the elements of a compelling soap opera: a star-studded squabble involving an apparently upstart subject put down by an implacable king.

Why had Godfrey chosen such a public format for LaRosa's ouster? "I had to fire him on the air," he reasoned later, "because I hired him on the air." Pressed for a further explanation, Godfrey told reporters that LaRosa had demonstrated an "improper lack of humility." There it was at last, the terrible crime: LaRosa apparently had not shown proper deference to the man who had discovered him.

Nevertheless, it was LaRosa to whom the public

offered its sympathy. The very idea—a nice young guy from Brooklyn, an ex-serviceman, everybody's kid brother, being humiliated on the air! And by a man who tendered himself as a friendly neighbor. The public was appalled—all the more so because LaRosa had only humble praise for his former boss.

Obviously, there was more to the firing than the version offered by Godfrey. What he had characterized as a lack of humility was more a matter of LaRosa's growing independence. As one of the regulars on *Arthur Godfrey and His Friends,* the singer had at first submitted to Godfrey's autocratic rule. Storm clouds began to gather when LaRosa bucked certain of the boss's commandments—such as using Godfrey's lawyer as his personal manager. (It was an unwritten law that performers would not "need" agents on the Godfrey show; financial arrangements for the regulars were made directly by Godfrey's producer and/or lawyer, without middlemen.) Then there was that little matter of the hit record LaRosa had released without asking his mentor's permission. Worst of all, LaRosa was emerging as the show's primary attraction: Possessed of a sweetly modest personality, he had a naiveté that immediately won over audiences. By the end of his second year with the show, the twenty-three-year-old LaRosa was on the receiving end of six thousand fan letters a week.

LaRosa might have gotten away with all this if only he had taken his place at the ballet barre. Another of Godfrey's whims, ballet lessons, had been prescribed for all the "little Godfreys." And in the beginning, the ex-Navy man dutifully submitted. But as others began to dodge the class, so, finally, did he. "Next morning I go in, I find a note: 'Since you felt your services weren't required at the ballet class yesterday, you won't be needed on tonight's show.'" Feeling the need of an advocate after Godfrey refused to discuss the matter, LaRosa went out and got an agent. This proved to be the last straw.

LaRosa went on to score appearances on Ed Sullivan's *Toast of the Town,* several hit records, and even a series of his own; but aside from a local radio show in New York, his career never really ignited again. As for Godfrey, the LaRosa firing would haunt him for the rest of his days. Not that he thereafter tempered his intemperate dealings with his cast and staff. "Remember that many of you are here over the bodies of people I have personally slain," he would growl at the little Godfreys. "I have done it before and I can do it again."

And that he did. After offing LaRosa he fired orchestra leader Archie Bleyer (who ran the record company that recorded LaRosa), producer Larry Puck, and the Chordettes. Both men had made the mistake of dating two of the Little Godfreys. The Chordettes apparently stepped on the boss's toes too, although they never knew how. Then in April 1955, in one fell swoop, Godfrey fired Marion Marlowe, Haleloke, and the Mariners, plus three writers. Although he replaced them practically on a one-for-one basis with sound-alike look-alikes, the show's family feeling was never quite the same again. Godfrey was able to keep both his morning and evening shows until he voluntarily decided to leave them, but their popularity in later days never matched that of the early fifties.

After a final season in a half-hour format in 1958–59 (and some strange behavior that included buzzing an airport control tower with his DC-3), Godfrey exited nighttime TV. He turned up briefly on *Candid Camera* in 1960–61, then moonlighted on radio, until his tearful farewell broadcast in 1972. Having survived a bout with cancer, he devoted himself primarily to conservationist causes in later years, limiting his TV appearances to commercial pitches for life insurance which he delivered, as always, in his patented folksy manner (while looking like Howdy Doody's very old daddy).

Postscript: Godfrey and LaRosa had a chance meeting on the street many years later in Manhattan. Godfrey held out his hands in a friendly greeting, and LaRosa in turn threw his arms around Godfrey in a warm embrace. "We'd better be careful," LaRosa said, "or the papers will make something out of this." "Fuck 'em, my boy," Godfrey replied.

It might not seem like such a big deal now that everything from live performances on the Grammys to the marching bands at the Macy's Thanksgiving Day Parade are prerecorded, but on the morning following star tenor Mario Lanza's much ballyhooed television debut on CBS's live variety special *The Shower of Stars* in 1953, the Associated Press revealed that the legendary Lanza had, in fact, been lip-synching an operatic aria off one of his old records. After issuing an official denial, CBS ultimately admitted the truth, revealing that Lanza had lost his voice owing to severe stage fright as well as a massive drop in weight following two weeks of crash dieting to get skinny for the show. The ensuing flap forced Lanza to hold a singing press conference to combat press accusations that he could no longer carry a tune.

In late December of 1952, the playwright and Algonquin Round Table regular George S. Kaufman said during a live broadcast of *This Is Show Business:* "Let's make this the one program on which no one sings 'Silent Night.'" CBS's switchboard lit up with calls like a veritable Christmas tree. Apparently, viewers construed the remark to be antireligious and, more specifically, anti-Christian, since it had been made by a Jew. Fearing a viewer boycott, CBS dropped Kaufman from the show amid considerable publicity. He was quietly reinstated once the ruckus died down.

What if there were no Vanna, no *Wheel,* no Wink, no dippy newlyweds, no Bachelor Number One? What dirt-cheap money-gushing filler would programmers use to replace game shows? The only thing cheaper and easier to produce is the test pattern. And yet the genre came very close to extinction in the late fifties when scandal banished the high-stakes thrillers into an isolation-booth limbo that lasted for several years. But the lure of watching plain folks get rich quick was an addiction the public was unable or unwilling to shake.

181

182

"Merely entertainment": **Hal March** hosted the ill-fated $64,000 Question.

The $64,000 Question was the one that made it all happen, the show that blasted quiz shows out of the category of throwaway diversions for bored housewives and into high-rated prime time. At the height of its popularity, the show won 85 percent of the viewing audience—edging *Lucy* out of the number-one slot for the first time. Showy and suspenseful, its format defied contestants to answer difficult questions on obscure subjects. The ante doubled with each correct response, and so did the tension, since a wrong answer meant forfeiting all winnings. Those contestants who made it to the $4,000 plateau could return each week thereafter with the option of facing another double-or-nothing question, up to the top prize of $64,000, or they could walk away with what they had already won. Viewers were mesmerized as Average Joes spouted arcane answers to questions on boxing, baseball, and Japanese history. They suffered along with the contestants who mopped their brows and covered their eyes, grimacing from the expenditure of mental effort. Windowed coffins dubbed "isolation booths" kept contestants from being distracted or helped by answers shouted by the audience.

Game shows were gladiatorial contests—the little man (or woman) against ever-mounting odds—that allowed millions of video voyeurs to imagine themselves up there on that stage, dazzling the country with their encyclopedic knowledge of bats or ballet. Psychologist Joyce Brothers was an expert on boxing; Redmond O'Hanlon was a cop who won $16,000 for his knowledge of Shakespeare; child actress Patty Duke was an expert on music. They all appeared on *The $64,000 Question*.

But perhaps the most famous—and later infamous—of all game show contestants was Charles Van Doren, a low-salaried college assistant professor who appeared on *Twenty-One* (a variation of *The $64,000 Question*) and, by sheer weight of intellect (it seemed), became something of a national hero, sort of an egghead Rocky. His isolation booth histrionics as he stammered and strained to call up his answers earned him winnings of $129,000 and a regular spot on the *Today* show.

Accusations of double dealing by quiz show producers first surfaced in 1957 when a man awaiting his turn on a show called *Dotto* discovered another contestant's notebook, which happened to contain all the answers to the questions she was just then being asked on the air. Though *Dotto*'s producers tried to buy him off (with a modest sum), he took his story to the New York State attorney general.

By 1959, the inquiry into the matter had mushroomed into a full-scale probe. One hundred and fifty witnesses were brought before a grand jury to answer questions about the prepping practices of quiz shows. The proceedings generated front-page coverage that caused even President Eisenhower, apparently a fan, to express his dismay.

Months of scrutiny followed by a Senate subcommittee investigation ultimately caused the quiz-show world's best-known winner, Charles Van Doren, to confess his own part in the deception. In a statement to the Senate subcommittee, he said:

> *[The producer] took me into his bedroom where we could talk alone. He told me that Herbert Stempel, the current champion, was an 'unbeatable' contestant because he knew too much. He said that Stempel was unpopular and was defeating opponents right and left to the detriment of the program. He asked me if, as a favor to him, I would agree to make an arrangement whereby I would tie Stempel and thus increase the entertainment value of the program.*
>
> *He also told me that the show was merely entertainment and that giving help to quiz contestants was a common practice and merely part of show business. This, of course, was not true, but I wanted to believe him. He also stressed the fact that by appearing on a nationally televised program, I would be doing a great service to the intellectual life, to teachers and to education in general, by increasing public respect for the work of the mind through my performances.*

Van Doren went on to say that after winning $129,000, he finally asked to be allowed to lose—and did so after another suitably engaging contestant was found to take his place.

Van Doren's confession rocked the country. Who could you believe if not a mild-mannered college prof? Although no punitive action was taken against him, Van Doren lost his spot on *Today* and his assistant professorship at Columbia. In all, one hundred witnesses were eventually shown to have lied to the grand jury—although only ten were indicted for perjury.

Instructed by her guardian and business manager John Ross to deny that she had been supplied with answers by the *$64,000 Question* show staff,

183

Patty Duke broke down under questioning during the Senate hearing. "Are you sure you've told us the truth?" Congressman Oren Harris asked her. "No sir, I have not," she heard herself replying. Viewed more as a victim than a co-conspirator, Patty herself didn't suffer any punishment; but her testimony was particularly damning for the show's producers, establishing, as she recalled later, that "not only had these people perpetrated a hoax on the public, but they'd gone so far as to use children to do it."

Game shows hadn't broken any laws—on the books, anyway. But though no evidence of cheating was ever found against it, *The $64,000 Question* was summarily cancelled. And when it was discovered that even *Queen for a Day* was rigged (the applause meter registered in favor of contestants who wanted a product the show could plug), the big-money game shows were bounced for several years.

The quiz show scandal marked the beginning of the end of TV's age of innocence. No longer would America believe just anything it saw on the tube.

The young Dick Clark had the sincere, well-scrubbed good looks of an emissary of the Campus Crusade for Christ when he broke through the public consciousness on *American Bandstand*. He exuded oceans of likability, but even then he was a manipulator with huge power. His power might have been even greater if not for those congressional investigations that brought on the payola scandal with its allegations of payoffs and gifts to disc jockeys in 1959.

The budding entrepreneur got into serious action a year after *Bandstand* went national in 1957 as he became more and more involved in the manufacture of pop recording stars. The market was his to exploit, what with rock's original roster of stars having been ravaged by untimely death (Buddy Holly, Eddie Cochran), scandal (Chuck Berry, Jerry Lee Lewis), and an ill-timed tour of army duty (Elvis). To fill the gap left by the genuine pioneers, Clark and his associates offered less menacing substitutes on the order of Frankie Avalon, Fabian, and Bobby Rydell—neighborhood Philly boys who'd been expressly packaged to meet the taste of *American Bandstand*'s after-school audience (as well as that of their folks). Clark's interest in these vacuous dreamboats may have been directed by more than just casual appreciation. He held a whole or part interest in thirty-three rock-'n'-roll-related businesses, including record and publishing companies, a management concern, and a record-pressing plant. He also promoted cross-coun-

Dick Clark once attributed part of his success as a teen host to a fortuitous lack of interest in younger women. Here the Perennial Teenager takes a break with two favorite "regulars," **Rosie** and **Franny**.

try tours of one-nighters under the banner "Dick Clark's Caravan of Stars" (although most of the headlines were paid anything but star wages). It was these extracurricular activities that were of particular interest to the Senate subcommittee.

"The senators were surprised to find out that there was so much money in pop music that I didn't need to be paid to play records. It was a shock to the political mind that I could accumulate great wealth in a short length of time without stealing." Ultimately, Clark's Young Republican good looks and earnest boy-next-door demeanor helped get him off the Senate subcommittee's hit list—although he didn't exactly get off scot-free. "ABC asked me to divest myself of my recording and publishing interests," Clark remembered, "which I did. Probably now that complex would be in excess of $20 million."

But to hard-core fans, Clark's crimes against rock 'n' roll are of a much subtler nature: Denying the spontaneity at the heart of the music, he insisted on a lip-sync policy for all the musical guests on *Ameri-*

can *Bandstand.* And then there was the cold shoulder he gave some of the giants of the era. Among the first to feel the chill was Jerry Lee Lewis, following his marriage to his thirteen-year-old cousin Myra. Clark also turned his back on Chuck Berry after his arrest for violating the Mann Act. Given *Bandstand's* enormous clout, the injury to those already misbegotten careers is unknowable and incalculable.

While the wholesome Clark got off with hardly a slap on the wrist, despite allegations of millions of dollars worth of conflicting interests, the earthier and more influential Alan Freed became, in effect, the payola squad's sacrificial lamb, taking the fall for an alleged $30,650 in kickbacks.

It took the Canadian Broadcasting Company to probe an issue that had only been whispered about for years concerning the treatment of animals on wildlife shows. The CBC's Cruel Camera showed scenes from the much-beloved series *Wild Kingdom,* which was broadcast regularly on NBC from 1968 to 1971, and which then moved into syndication, with new episodes produced through 1978. It turns out, however, that *Wild Kingdom's* cameras were not quite as candid as its viewers were led to believe. For example, how did the bear they rescued from a swamp come to be there in the first place? Someone from the show pushed him in—scaring him half to death—that's how. And how do you get an alligator to attack a water moccasin? Tie a string to the snake's tail and throw him into the water in range of the alligator, then reel him back in. Do this often enough and the alligator will attack the snake out of sheer boredom or exasperation.

185

Marlin Perkins convinces an unwilling armadillo to make his television debut.

In 1964, when Jackie Mason was in his thirties, he stood on the brink of superstardom; but the ground gave way with the wiggle of a single finger—his. Mason was in the middle of his stand-up act one Sunday night on *The Ed Sullivan Show* when, off-camera, Sullivan held up two fingers, a signal that Mason had two minutes left in his allotted segment. Mason, on a roll with the audience, responded with a finger signal of his own. Whether or not it was obscene—and Mason contended it was not—Sullivan took offense and proceeded to vilify Mason in the press. A subsequent libel suit brought by Mason was decided in his favor after a New York Supreme Court judge viewed a clip of the show and ruled that he saw "nothing offensive" in Jackie's performance. But

Jackie Mason in happier times during the run of The World According to Me.

such was Sullivan's power that Jackie Mason was nevertheless branded an outcast, at least in terms of television work. He spent more than twenty years in a kind of show-business limbo—working the Catskill mountain resorts and the gambling circuit.

"I never starved," he says now. "I worked. I always worked. Miami. Vegas. Atlantic City. I made $500,000 a year. Some years I made close to a million. But this is the only business in the world [in which] if you make $20,000 a week, you're a pathetic failure."

Four years after declaring bankruptcy because he'd invested all his money in plays and movies that failed, Mason's one-man show *The World According to Me* became a Broadway hit, winning him financial success and a Tony. The show ran for a couple of years—with the high point of the evening being Mason's imitation of Ed Sullivan.

Just as he had always insisted he should be, he became a superstar, complete with an ABC sitcom, *Chicken Soup,* that was built around his act. But just as the show was being launched, Mason once again managed to shoot himself in the foot. Riding the wave of popularity as a New York home boy made good, he became the unlikely campaign sidekick of poker-faced New York mayoral candidate Rudolph Giuliani, for whom he provided much needed comic relief. But Mason made one quip too many when he cracked that black mayoral candidate David Dinkins looked "like a black model without a job," and then added insult to injury by declaring that Jewish support for Dinkins was based on Jewish guilt. The following week brought another disastrous flurry of headlines when *Newsweek* magazine quoted him as calling Dinkins a "schvartzer," a Yiddish term with racially pejorative connotations.

Within a few days, Mason was forced to withdraw from the campaign. And not many weeks later, he was forced to withdraw from TV—although not necessarily because the country disapproved of what might be considered racial slurs. Deep down inside middle America might even have agreed with his sentiments. No, it was Jackie they couldn't take. But then, the idea of formulating a sitcom around a comedian with Yiddish intonations, clipped sentences, and machine-gun delivery had always been a gamble. Jackie was—and is—basically a New York phenomenon, and it was there he would stay—an unofficial mayor who continues to hold court at the Stage Deli despite this latest setback in a long and controversial career.

She was a famous flake; the inspiration for several of Woody Allen's flakiest screen characters; a legendary neurotic who had spent the week prior to hosting a 1976 *Saturday Night Live* crawling around the NBC hallways on her hands and knees, and who had, twenty minutes before she was scheduled to go on the air, locked herself in her dressing room and refused to come out. Insecure, brilliant, and often unintentionally funny, Louise Lasser *was Mary Hartman, Mary Hartman.*

Any doubt about that was dispelled when the landmark sitcom incorporated Lasser's much-publicized arrest in a Beverly Hills boutique into its already bizarre plotline. That arrest had occurred after police entered the boutique following an altercation between Lasser and a salesperson, and Lasser astonished everyone by lying down next to a doll house and refusing to budge—apparently her idea of passive resistance. A subsequent search of her purse revealed a tiny vial of cocaine. (She later said a fan had given it to her.)

Forget about waxy yellow buildup—Mary/Louise hadn't known what heartache was till she found herself caught up in the middle of a real-life scandal. The arrest made headlines all over the country as front pages shouted that Mary Hartman had been busted. After spending a few hours in jail, Lasser explained to reporters that she had a blood infection and a 102-degree fever. She had also been having trouble distinguishing between Mary's character and her own, it seems. Playing off that strong character identification, Lasser, as Mary, recreated the now famous doll house incident (minus the cocaine). And a few weeks later, with pressures building up on the show as well as in Lasser's not so private life, Mary Hartman had a nervous breakdown—causing millions of viewers to wonder just who was cracking up before their eyes: Mary or Louise Lasser.

A funny thing happened to Morton Downey, Jr., on his slide from the top of the TV heap: Somebody drew a swastika on his forehead—or rather, a mirror image of one. And therein lay the problem. The controversy generated by this peculiar incident backfired on him, eroding what little credibility he still had with the public.

Downey wasn't the first "confrontational" TV host to bait his guests and browbeat his audiences. He might not even have been the most obnoxious; after all, his predecessors include the vicious Joe Pine, the thickheaded Alan Burke, and the insolent Les Crane. Pine expired of his own bile, Burke slipped back into anonymity, and Crane went on to found a multimillion-dollar software company, leaving Downey to suffer the most humiliating fall from grace of all.

Downey had cut through America's consciousness with all the subtlety of a chainsaw, presiding over his syndicated talk show like some cap-toothed soapbox orator, bellowing his own distinctive version of insults and right-wing cant at friend and foe alike. "Zip it, fathead," he commanded the "pablum-puking bleeding hearts" who didn't share his antigay, antiminority, anticommunist, antieverything prejudices. Much of Downey's histrionics were pure show biz, and yet bottled up inside him was an authentic rage that endeared him to the studio audiences of wild-eyed meatheads who egged him on. Mort was mad as hell and wasn't gonna take it anymore!

But when all was shouted and done, Mort had a limited amount of shtick; and once the shock value wore off, he had little to say. In the spring of 1989, with his ratings slipping badly, he took to the road on a publicity tour to rejuvenate his anemic ratings. It was then, in a San Francisco airport restroom, that he supposedly encountered the roving band of neo-Nazi skinheads who clipped his hair and decorated his skull with a swastika.

The story generated headlines all over the country, but there were a few troubling inconsistencies in Downey's tale. A fifteen-year-old who'd been in the area of the bathroom at the time told police he had seen no skinheads. And then, too, the swastika was backwards—just as it would have been if Downey had drawn it on himself while looking in the mirror. To compound the confusion, the San Francisco police said the mark on Downey's face at the time he first reported the incident did not match the one in later photographs.

In a special show devoted to his colleague's troubles, Phil Donahue told Downey, "I believe you." Unfortunately for Downey, the San Francisco police—and the public—apparently did not.

187

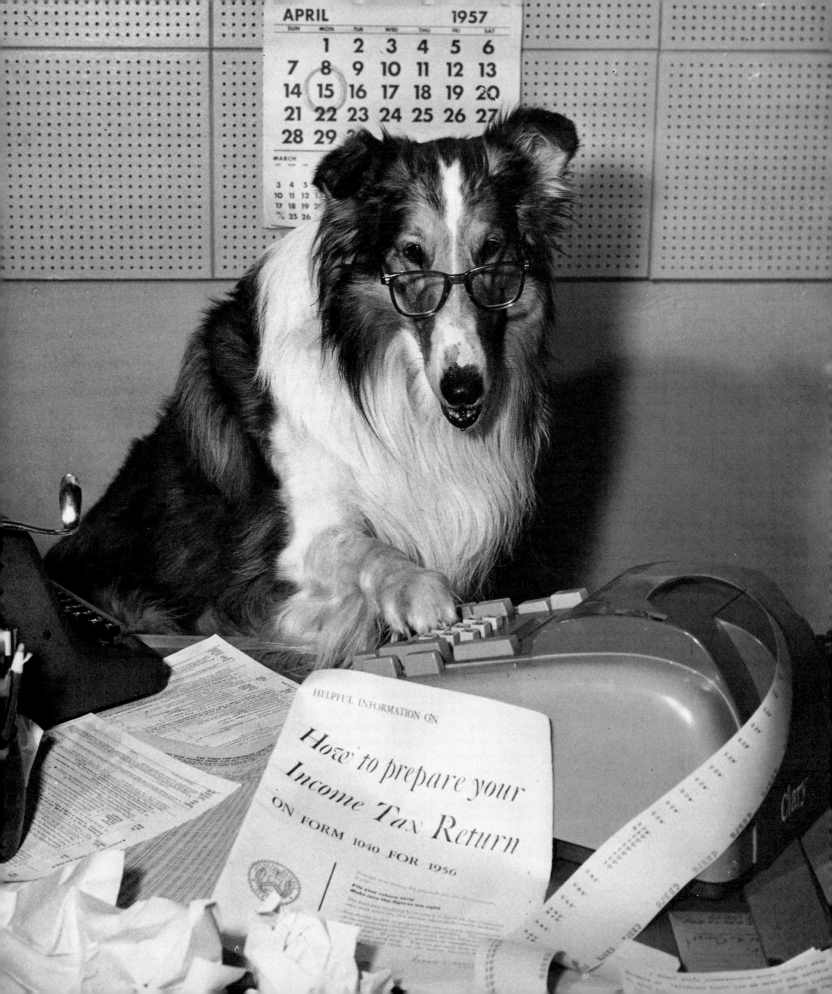

HOW TO BE A TV STAR

Black Saturday. September 3, 1977. Mary Richards throws her hat into the air for the last time, and a nation weeps.

She could turn the world on with her smile. She could take a routine sitcom formula and make it all seem worthwhile. Mary Tyler Moore left such an indelible impression as Laura Petrie and Mary Richards that the public has never really accepted her as anything—or anyone—else, including her own complicated real-life self. In the years since *The Mary Tyler Moore Show* has been off the air, she's done everything but go door-to-door in her quest to win her way back into our hearts. But we've never really let her come home. It's not that we don't love her; it's just that we love her early TV alter ego so much more.

Mary's not the first to find out that this TV-star thing can be a trap, to discover that television's ubiquity stamps an oft-irrevocable identity on an actor. Unlike movie stars, with whom we rendezvous on giant screens in darkened theaters, TV stars come right into our homes, sometimes two or three times a day. They're there with us when we eat, brush our teeth, get dressed, and engage in heaven-knows-what other intimate activities. It is any wonder, then, that the actors who play these parts end up shrinking to fit their small-screen identities? Once cast in the public mind, so shall they ever remain. Shirley Booth, the distinguished Oscar and Tony award-winning actress, became so connected with the part of Hazel, the sitcom maid, that for years afterward she got letters requesting cleaning tips. And though Robert Young no longer makes house calls as Marcus Welby, fans still collar him on the street to ask for medical advice.

It took a nude scene (with Jeff Bridges in *Stay Hungry*) to liberate Sally Field from her icky-sweet image as the Flying Nun. By getting down and dirty in serious roles in movies like *Norma Rae,* Sally finally managed to transcend her television persona. It hasn't been nearly that easy for others. Farrah Fawcett, for example, was perfectly willing to shed her clothes and makeup in her first few films if only she could shed her bimbo Angel image along with them;

but her career floundered miserably until she returned to the small screen, where she belongs. Farrah is now the star of choice for all those reality-based made-for-TV movies. And at that she's plenty lucky: it can be (and often is) worse for series stars who jump ship to "stretch" as an actor (i.e., to scream their heads off) and "grow" into more demanding big-screen roles—only to end up vanishing completely. (Michael Parks, phone home.)

The predictability of the way in which TV shows are packaged has a way of imprisoning actors and denaturing even the most compelling personalities. In pandering to the public's love of the familiar, TV recycles its own formulas over and over; once an actor clicks with a particular bit of business (like the Fonz's "A-a-a-a-a" greeting), it's milked until the public gets sick of it. And yet, they won't allow the star to do anything else. In that respect, TV can be even crueler than the old studio system. Contract players may have been forced to make as many as six pictures a year during the days of assembly line production in Hollywood, but at least some often got a chance to break out of stereotypes by playing a variety of characters.

When Carroll O'Connor tried to return to the Broadway stage in a downbeat drama called *Brothers,* the New York critics dismissed it and him as Archie Bunker without the laughs. But instead of bellyaching about it, O'Connor went back to series TV for *In the Heat of the Night*—where his cracker sheriff (in the beginning, at least) was Archie Bunker transplanted down south. Sometimes playing variations on a single theme is the only way to go for actors who have had monumental success in a role. Ask Andy Griffith, whose Ben Matlock is Sheriff Andy Taylor dressed up as a folksy lawyer; or Raymond Burr, whose Ironsides was really just Perry Mason in a wheelchair.

Of course, this kind of thing can get out of hand. *Life With Lucy*'s rehash of the old *I Love Lucy* shenanigans was so shameless that one critic called it "Death With Lucy." And yet it's not as if the public would have accepted Lucille Ball as anything but a Lucy-Ricardo style cutup. "I've been trying to do

189

something that people would believe and buy," Ball said at the time. "Well, they didn't buy it. What the people seem to want is Lucy. So I'm doing Lucy." Which didn't satisfy the public, either—for not only was this last, ill-fated show too cynically derivative of the original, but it had also become all but impossible for audiences to buy the idea of this ancient, enormously wealthy businesswoman with a loving cup stuck on her head. It was far more satisfying to watch the vintage Lucy in rerun.

For even the greatest stars, demythification is the downside of TV stardom. Yet the rewards—the endorsements, the obligatory record-album deal, and the box on *The Hollywood Squares* (not to mention

the tendency to become very, very rich)—do a lot to compensate them for their plight. And when the long run is ended and they've looked into the camera and gurgled or gasped or done a spit-take for the very last time, they can walk away secure in the knowledge that they can still run for president—or for mayor of Palm Springs. Or should they so desire, they can just keep doing the same thing in one series after another until the variations sound the right theme again. Sure, Mary Tyler Moore will forever be identified with Mary Richards in the public consciousness; but she can do a new series every year, if she (and her production company) are of a mind. Yes indeed . . . she can do it over and over till she gets it right.

What They Don't Tell You in TV Star School . . .

NO MATTER WHAT IT IS, TAKE THE PART! Everybody's gotta start somewhere. Everybody's gotta have a place to be bad. For countless stars, that place has been TV. Play the part of a flying nun marooned on a desert island with a talking horse if it's offered, and stay with it till there are enough episodes (ideally one hundred) to make a juicy syndication deal.

HANG IN (NO MATTER HOW BORED YOU ARE). After six years of playing Lorne Greene's son on the long-running series *Bonanza,* Pernell Roberts quit to "teach Hollywood a lesson about junk TV." Instead, TV taught him a lesson about the bottom line. He spent the next fourteen years starring in regional theater productions and doing occasional TV guest spots. His departure from the Adam Cartwright role is estimated to have cost him more than a million dollars in residual earnings. Sadder but wiser (and balder), Roberts finally resurfaced in Seriesland in 1979 as Trapper John, M.D.

NO MATTER HOW MUCH ATTENTION YOU GET, YOU'RE STILL EXPENDABLE—at least as far as the bigwigs are concerned. *Dukes of Hazzard* heartthrobs Tom Wopat and John Schneider found that out the hard way when they were replaced by two look-alikes after demanding a raise and a fair share of millions of dollars' worth of *Dukes* merchandise. Leonard Nimoy got the message when he made a stink about getting a phone in his *Star Trek* dressing room and a producer told him that if he didn't back off, they'd "put the ears on somebody else."

BEHAVE YOURSELF! Okay, so Roseanne Barr wrested control of her show by staging a coup against her producer, but that's not the way it usually works. Cybill Shepherd won the battle with *Moon-*

lighting's creator, Glenn Scott Caron, only to lose the war after he stormed out and serious script rot set in.

ATTRACT THE RIGHT FANS. In this, the era of so-called "narrow casting," your ratings can be anemic so long as the viewers you attract are the kind who buy foreign cars and designer deodorant. (That's how Don Johnson managed to hang out on the beach for five years.) But if you attract the wrong fans, even critical acclaim and high ratings may not save you.

EXPLOIT YOUR REPUTATION. Part of the recompense for being a TV star are the sweet endorsement deals. They're so sweet, in fact, that they're often more lucrative for stars than their acting careers. James Garner's Polaroid commercials with Mariette Hartley spanned a longer period of time than any of his series.

Who knows how long it'll be before you've worn out your welcome with viewers? Take advantage while you can: Lend your name to a line of K-Mart fashions or a diet drink; push white wine, red meat, or aspirin.

Think of Farrah Fawcett, who by the second season of *Charlie's Angels* had redefined the parameters of sudden celebrity with $17 million in endorsements: $4.5 million from Fabergé, another million for a three-hour photo session to advertise a faucet-shaped necklace, and several million more in pocket change from tee-shirts, posters, lunch pails, and dolls.

If the commercial suits you well enough, it might just give your career a second wind. Look at Bill Cosby. His cutesy-poo Jell-O pudding commercials were spun off into a cutesy-poo television show. His success on the show then made his endorsement deals even more profitable. His going rate is about $125,000 an hour—a million dollars a day. Thanks to Jell-O, Mattel, Kodak, and Coke, he's estimated to have made $60 mil in 1989 alone. And that doesn't include the earnings from his books, which are spin-offs of the image perpetrated first by the commercials, then by the show. 1986's *Fatherhood* was the fastest selling book in the history of publishing, with earnings of $1.7 mil in hardcover alone. In 1989, Cosby brought out yet another tome—*Love and Marriage.* (Golly, the way he cranks these books out, what with his series and commercials and concert dates, you'd almost think he didn't write them himself.) Some say that Dr. Cosby has taken this sort of thing too far—such as when he sang the praises of E. F. Hutton, the financial-services company that had earlier pleaded guilty to charges of fraud. Yes, Cosby

is the only star who runs the risk of giving overexposure a bad name.

But don't you worry about overexposure or selling out; by the time you're big enough to be offered an endorsement deal, it will already be too late.

DON'T BE PICKY. Think of Morgan Fairchild waxing ecstatic about cubic zirconias on an extended commercial format that fools you into thinking it's a talk show, and of John Ritter extolling the virtues of home correspondence courses. Consider Martha Raye and June Allyson, who told us more than we wanted to know about their personal hygiene with their ads for Polident and Depends. Speaking of "The Big Mouth," make sure your image matches the product you're trying to push: Remember how uncomfortable John Houseman looked selling Puritan Oil and Big Macs.

Take a cue from Joan Collins, who's sold her name to everyone from Jack LaLanne to a rubber-rose manufacturer. Joan's ex-husband Anthony Newley says she'd sell her own bowel movement if she thought someone would buy it. (And Bill Cosby would probably do the commercials if the money was right.)

BE DISCREET. In 1987, as part of a $29 million campaign to get Americans back into eating red meat, Cybill Shepherd munched a hamburger on TV in behalf of the Beef Association of America. But later that same year, she absentmindedly listed "cutting out fatty foods" and "staying away from red meat" as being among her special beauty secrets in *Family Circle* magazine. Oops. In a second unfortunate setback for the Beef Association, James Garner, another of its spokespersons, underwent open heart surgery while his "real food for real people" commercials were in heavy TV rotation.

In 1986 Seagram's gave Bruce Willis $7 million for eight super-cool commercials to push its Golden Wine Cooler. Within four months of their airing, its sales had quadrupled. Even so, Seagram's had second thoughts about using Bruce after stories of his boozy brawls began hitting the papers.

CHOOSE YOUR PRODUCT WISELY. In a 1990 ruling, a California judge found that celebrities could be held liable for misrepresentations when endorsing a product or service. The suit had been brought against Lloyd Bridges by investors bilked by two Michigan-based mortgage companies whose investment products he'd hawked in television ads.

Oh, and a few other things . . .

191

Just Starting Out?

**Do Whatever It Takes To Get
Yourself Noticed . . .**

Goldie Hawn on Laugh-In

**(Don't Worry—Your Fans Will
Forgive Or Forget)**

Get Yourself a Gimmick

Edd "Kookie" Byrnes

Don Adams in Get Smart

Sally Field in The Flying Nun

Lily Tomlin on Laugh-In

193

Or a Compelling Co-Star

Lassie and Jon Provost

194

Robert Blake and friend

Getting a Little Stale?
Play Against Type

Betty White on The Mary Tyler Moore Show and The Golden Girls

or Play It Safe . . . Play Yourself

Tony Randall as Felix Unger in The Odd Couple

A Tad Overweight?
Make a Profession of Being Fat

Jackie

If You're a Child Star,
Be Terminally Cute

Emmanuel Lewis

(And Never, Ever Grow Up)

196

Roseanne

Do Absolutely Nothing Extremely Well

Garry Moore

Vanna White

Bert Parks

Abandon All Semblance of Dignity or Taste . . .

Red Skelton

198

Be Queen for a Day . . .

Robert Vaughn in Hotel

Conrad Bain in Diff'rent Strokes

Don Knotts in The Andy Griffith Show

Ted Bessell with Marlo Thomas in That Girl

Sorrell Booke and James Best in The Dukes of Hazzard

Peter Kastner in The Ugliest Girl in Town

200

Flip Wilson with Carol Channing on The Flip Wilson Show

John Ritter in Three's Company

201

Tom Hanks in Bosom Buddies

Jamie Farr in M*A*S*H

Bruce Weitz in Hill Street Blues

If Something Works,

Do It Again

I Love Lucy

And Again

Here's Lucy

Give Your Best, But Be Prepared to Burn Out Fast (Your Fans Will Stay Faithful Even If You Never Again Attain the Quality of Your Early Work)

203

Milton Berle

And Again

Life With Lucy

Take Advantage of Your TV Q (Quick Before It Melts)

Cut a Record

Patty Duke

Write a Book

Vanna Speaks

Merchandise Yourself

Walt Disney

Elizabeth Montgomery reads the popular new Bewitched comic book.

Make a Movie

Bruce Willis in Die Hard

206

Any Movie

Lisa Bonet in Angel Heart

Go Legit

Lucy in <u>Wildcat</u>

Farrah Fawcett in <u>Extremities</u>

Quit While You're at the Top of Your Game . . .

![Mary Tyler Moore with Ed Asner in The Mary Tyler Moore Show]

Mary Tyler Moore with Ed Asner in The Mary Tyler Moore Show

It was easy to see the plucky Mary Richards as an extension of the character Mary Tyler Moore had played on *The Dick Van Dyke Show*—to imagine her as Laura Petrie striking out on her own. So it must have seemed logical to her and her comedy brain trust to once again revive the Laura/Mary character when she returned to sitcom land for the third time as *Mary.* But this time around there was no growth for Mary's character. Aside from the fact that she played a divorced woman, this new Mary wasn't new at all. She worked at a midwestern paper as its "Helpline" columnist; her newsroom cronies included her boss (a cranky but good-hearted man's man), a wise-cracking best girlfriend, and a blowhard drama critic. (Sound familiar?) As for Mary, she was still an ingenue—albeit an extremely mature ingenue.

Not only was *Mary* a lackluster rehash of Moore's previous sitcom, but its creators had neglected to factor their star's stormy private life into the Laura/Mary mythology. That created a problem, since by then Mary's ill health, personal traumas, and family tragedies had become a staple of the tabloids and supermarket slicks. We knew if she got a hickey—sometimes before she did. Mary could no longer pull off the innocent with the tremulous voice. She'd outgrown plucky little Mary Richards.

Then Return in a Wimpy Version of the Hit That Made You a Name

Mary Tyler Moore with James Farentino in Mary

1987's *Annie McGuire* attempted to let Mary grow up—with what Moore described as "a very human character . . . who has stains on her dress, who screws things up . . . and who has a sexual vitality that needs to be paid attention to." Sexual? Well, maybe; *sexy,* certainly. Even the rather prim Mary Richards was on the Pill. (We'd found out when her parents came to check up on her in Minneapolis, remember?) But screw things up? It just doesn't figure. Mary now has such authority that she can't be comfortably contained by routine sitcom nonsense. There's no way we'll ever again believe that this fiercely impressive woman would ever cook a pot roast—let alone burn it.

For now, it seems the only answer is for Mary to play an extremely rich, extremely thin TV star—who can't quite get her new series to work. The supporting cast would include her extremely rich ex-husband the TV mogul and a gang of neurotic but lovable Jewish writers* who try to come up with a winning premise for her week after week.

Whatever she chooses to do, let's hope it happens soon. It's lonely without her.

* None of whom are played by McLean Stevenson.

Bide Your Time on the Small Screen Until Something Better (or Almost as Good) Comes Along

Season's Greetings from **Ronald Reagan,** the host of <u>The General Electric Theatre.</u>

No wonder **Ricky Nelson** isn't concentrating on script changes with his father and brother David; he's caught the eye of the lovely pigtailed actress standing with Don DeFore in the doorway of a portable dressing room on the set of The Adventures of Ozzie and Harriet (1953).

Mel Brooks (on floor) manages to break up his boss **Sid Caesar** and his guest stars **Art Carney** and **Audrey Meadows** during a Your Show of Shows rehearsal session. Not nearly so amused are Mel's writer colleagues **Mel Tolken** and **Woody Allen** (1952).

Long before **Elizabeth Montgomery** became a bewitching blond, she appeared on her father's pioneering dramatic anthology series, Robert Montgomery Presents (1952).

211

Who's the Boss? **Lucy** cracks up **Desi** on the set of I Love Lucy.

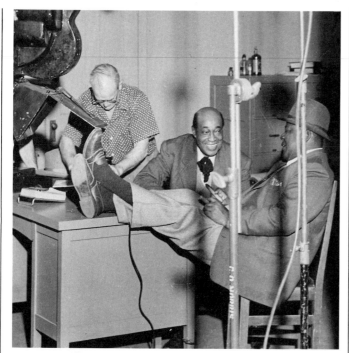

Tim "Kingfish" **Moore** enjoys a break with **Spencer Williams** on the set of Amos 'n' Andy. Although no whites appeared on the show, plenty worked behind the scenes.

212

Marilyn Monroe, at the height of her fame, makes her official TV debut on The Jack Benny Show in a sketch that would be revamped for her rival Jayne Mansfield several years later.

Audrey Meadows tries to focus **Jackie Gleason**'s short attention span on the script for this week's episode of The Honeymooners.

Jane Wyman with Bill Goodwin during the first year (1955) of what would become a long association with The Fireside Theatre, later The Jane Wyman Show.

Bright young comic **Johnny Carson** goes out of his way to accommodate Life of Riley star **William Bendix,** who's making a guest appearance on his new comedy variety show (1955).

The rapport between **Bill Cosby** and **Robert Culp** that sparked the adventure series I Spy extended off-screen as well.

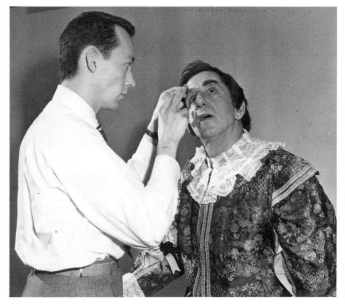

Jimmy Durante is readied for the role he was born to play —Cyrano. The Jimmy Durante Show (1954).

214

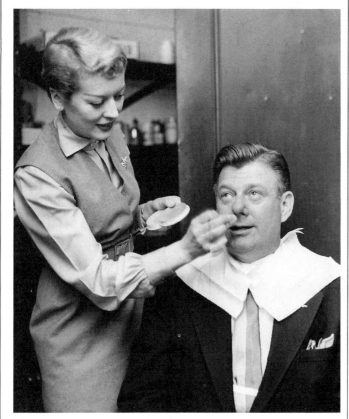

Makeup wizard Margot Kingsley touches up the Old Redhead's porcine nostrils before a broadcast of Arthur Godfrey's Talent Scouts (1955).

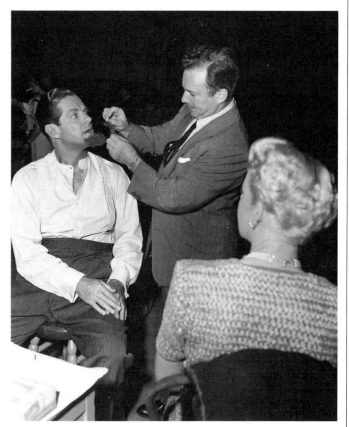

A fake beard gives Love That Bob **Cummings** a chance to display his versatility in another hilarious role change for his weekly comedy series. Guest star Virginia Fields looks on.

Mary Martin, the beloved star of Peter Pan, prepares for her network takeoff.

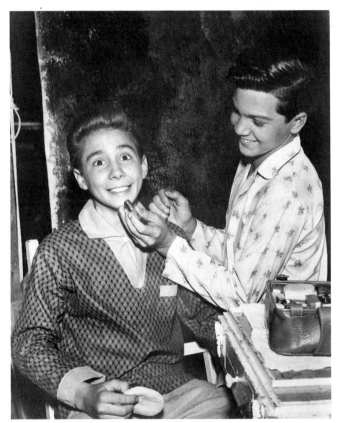

Dig those pompadours: **Johnny Crawford,** young star of The Rifleman, takes time out from a guest appearance on The Donna Reed Show to clown around with series regular **Paul Petersen.**

The illusion of facial perfection is carefully maintained for two stars of Charlie's Angels, **Farrah Fawcett** and **Kate Jackson.**

216

The rarely seen serious side of **Gracie Allen** can be glimpsed as she and husband **George Burns** wait for a shot to be prepped by the crew of The George Burns and Gracie Allen Show.

Two legends meet: **Mr. Ed** takes **Mae West** up on her invitation to ''come up and see me some time.''

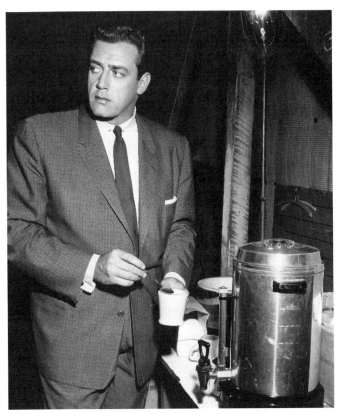

A strong defense requires strong coffee, according to Perry Mason's **Raymond Burr**.

Patty Duke makes like Liz as she studies her lines for a send-up of the much-talked-about film Cleopatra on The Patty Duke Show.

217

Gary Burghoff suns his cherubic face between takes on the set of M*A*S*H.

William Boyd celebrates a birthday with his wife, Grace Bradley, and the gang at Hopalong Cassidy (1949).

218

Ed Sullivan is caught happily musing over a milestone: His Toast of the Town is celebrating its seventh anniversary (1955).

Soupy Sales celebrates his show's first anniversary with a pastry confection too fabulous to throw.

The birdlike **Mia Farrow** doesn't have to worry about counting calories as she celebrates her nineteenth birthday on the set of Peyton Place. By the way, Mia's extreme new haircut is her own handiwork.

Richard Deacon prepares to take it on the chin from **Carl Reiner** on the set of The Dick Van Dyke Show.

"LEAVE IT TO BEAVER"

Jerry Mathers studies with his tutor as required by California law.

Donna Reed is as perfect as ever on the set of her popular sitcom.

220

Pausing with the intensely alert **Loretta Young** between takes on her dramatic anthology series are co-stars William Campbell (seated) and Bruce Bennett.

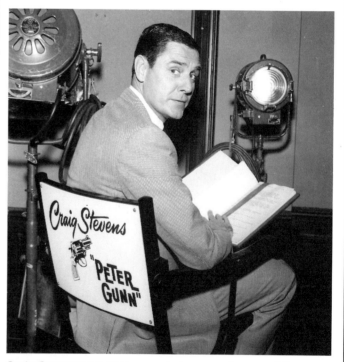

Craig Stevens practices nonchalance on the set of Peter Gunn.

Happy times for **Clint** ''Rowdy Yates'' **Eastwood**—a visit from his wife, Maggie, on the set of <u>Rawhide</u>.

221

Walt Disney shows one of the most popular stars of <u>The Mickey Mouse Club</u> some of the fan mail he's received from boys and girls all over the country.

Just Say No: **Nancy Reagan** makes a guest appearance (portraying herself) with **Gary Coleman** on <u>Diff'rent Strokes</u>.

Dinah Shore

222

Mwah!